Robert Christiansen Jr.
TRUE CRIME

California
Justice

California
Justice

Shootouts, Lynchings and Assassinations
in the Golden State

By
David Kulczyk

**Word
Dancer
Press**

Sanger, California

Printed in the United States of America.

Published by
Quill Driver Books/Word Dancer Press, Inc.,
1254 Commerce Ave, Sanger, CA 93657
559-876-2170 / 800-497-4909
QuillDriverBooks.com

Word Dancer Press books may be purchased for educational, fund-raising, business or promotional use. Please contact Special Markets, Quill Driver Books/ Word Dancer Press, Inc. at the above address or phone numbers.

Quill Driver Books/Word Dancer Press Project Cadre:
Doris Hall, David Marion, Stephen Blake Mettee, Carlos Olivas

ISBN 1-884995-54-3 • 978-1884955-54-5

**To order a copy of this book, please call
1-800-497-4909.**

Library of Congress Cataloging-in-Publication Data

Kulczyk, David.
  California justice : shootout, lynchings, and assasinations in the Golden State / by David Kulczyk.
    p. cm.
  Includes bibliographical references and index.
  ISBN-13: 978-1-884995-54-5 (pbk.)
  ISBN-10: 1-884995-54-3 (pbk.)
  1. Violent crimes—California—History—Case studies. 2. Lynching—California—History—Case studies. I. Title.
  HV6793.C2K85 2007
  364.1509794—dc22

                                                                        2007022539

This book is dedicated to my wife, Donna.

Chapter 8, *False Friends in Germantown*, was first published as
The Germantown Case of 1878—With Friends Like That
in the Spring 2006 issue of *Wagon Wheels*, the journal of the
Colusa [CA] County Historical Society, Volume 56, Number 1.

Contents

Acknowledgments

I would like to thank Eric Schumacher-Rasmussen for editing the manuscript and giving much needed words of advice and encouragement. I'd also like to thank everyone at the California State Library, the Sacramento Public Library and the Sacramento Room; Michael Hendryx and Dick Terwilliger at the Siskiyou County Museum; Susan Rawlins of the Colusa County Library; Joyce Johnson of the Humboldt County Library; Ruth Straessler of the Santa Rosa Convention & Visitors Bureau; Roberta L. Harlan of the Sonoma County Museum; Sandy Soeth of the Glenn County Board of Supervisors; Gene H. Russell, editor of *Wagon Wheels*, Colusa County Historical Society; Jonathan Pollack and Bill Colby of Madison Area Technical College; Jason Newman of Cosumnes River College; John Russell, Brett Lemke, Melinda Welsh, Tom Walsh, Bill Foreman, Steven T. Jones, Lorraine Clarke, Jackson Griffith, Jennifer Lewi, Dan Trocha, Rökker, and Steve Mettee.

Introduction

There have been thousands of books written and movies made about taking the law into one's own hands. The storyline almost always follows the same basic arc:

1. Bad guys abuse good guys.
2. Good guys attempt to take the high road until bad guys do something heinous enough that a) the good guys won't take it anymore, and b) the reader or audience is convinced that even the most committed pacifist would respond with violence.
3. Good guys pick off bad guys, one by one, in increasingly dramatic fashion.

These kinds of dramas are great escapism. Who hasn't wanted to stand up against a bully to protect life, family, or dignity? In real life, though, homemade justice is never so black-and-white. It is splattered with blood, brains, and fecal matter. The death groans of the wounded, or the sound of a person strangled to death, linger in the memories of the assailants until the day they die.

Anyone who has traveled widely through the state of California knows just how isolated many areas of the state are. With a population estimated in 2003 at 35,484,453, with 158,402 square miles of land, and with 840 miles of coastline, California could be considered a significant country of its own. While modern technology has reduced the isolation factor considerably, this certainly doesn't mean that California justice has always been dependent on law enforcement.

This book is by no means the "be-all to end-all" encyclopedia of shootouts, lynchings, and assassinations in California. Between 1849 and 1853, there were more than two hundred known cases of lynchings. There have been

A Californian about to pay the ultimate penalty in this undated photo. *(California State Library Photograph Collection)*

countless incidents of vigilantism throughout the history of California, but there exist few written accounts of these incidents. Most lynchings were committed by cowards who kept quiet, willing to take a life but unable to stomach the thought of a stay in San Quentin.

If a historian were to write a complete record of every shootout, lynching, and assassination that occurred in California, the book would be the size of the Los Angeles County phone book and only slightly more readable. This book is merely a snapshot of desperate events that led to drastic conclusions.

In the 1800s, Native Americans and Californios were gunned down like ducks and strung up like deer by the Anglos. Before the invasion of non-natives, California was a virtual paradise for the people living here. A pleasant climate, a variety of plants, and plenty of fish and game made life fairly easy for the natives. The tribes bartered and intermarried with each other, and violent conflict of any kind was relatively rare. But once the Spaniards arrived in California, life as the natives knew it was over. They were enslaved by the Spanish, then by the Mexicans, and finally they were virtually exterminated by the Caucasians. The Native Americans of California were hunted down and slaughtered like animals. Thousands were assassinated or lynched for no reason other than the color of their skin. For instance, in the spring of 1863, a group of ranchers from Butte County lost some of their horses and immediately blamed the loss on Natives Americans. They captured the first Native Americans that they found and hung them from a large oak tree in Helltown. The next day, the horses—which had merely wandered off to forage in the hills—came walking back to their barns.

Until the mid 1970s, a Yuba City tavern proudly displayed a large photo of dozens of Native Americans hanging by their necks from a tree, like a macabre Christmas tree.

The San Francisco vigilance committees of 1851 and 1856 were successful examples of democracy-at-work with the citizenry of the city establishing a phantom government in place of the ultra-corrupt official one that allowed connected criminals and politicians to commit murder, robbery, and assault with no fear of incarceration. Known criminals were put on notice to leave the city or face the consequences of California justice. Those who didn't leave were hanged, beaten, or shot. Law and order quickly came to San Francisco, but within a few years corruption slinked back in to "Baghdad by the Bay."

In 1856, King James of William, the founder and editor of San Francisco's stinging newspaper the *San Francisco Bulletin,* was shot on

A huge crowd showed up for the legal execution of Jose Forner on December 10, 1852, on San Francisco's Russian Hill. Not all hangings were of the illegal kind in early California. *(California State Library Photograph Collection)*

Montgomery Street by crooked city supervisor James P. Casey. Casey, a longtime fixer of elections, had won his board of supervisors seat with more votes than there were registered voters. The *Bulletin* exposed the crime and also pointed out that Casey had once been an inmate at New York state's notorious Sing Sing correctional facility. San Francisco police took Casey into custody, but the public distrusted the police department, knowing that cronyism would soon allow Casey back on the streets or, worse, allow him to skip town. Days before the King James of William assassination, gambler Charles Cora shot down unarmed United States Marshal William Richardson in cold blood. The good working people of San Francisco had had enough of the chaos caused by a protected class of criminals and a Second Committee of Vigilance was formed after King James of William passed away as a result of his gunshot wound.

On May 18, 1856, over three thousand volunteers marched in military formation to the city jail and demanded the surrender of Cora and Casey to the Committee of Vigilance, which had a total membership of over eight thousand armed men. The sheriff, knowing that he was vastly outnumbered, submitted to their demands and released Cora and Casey into the custody of the committee members.

The men were taken to a building that the committee had commandeered at Sacramento Street near Montgomery and there they were put on trial. Cora and Casey were deprived of outside counsel, but were assigned committee-appointed attorneys to represent them. The men made fruitless defense claims, but they were quickly found guilty and were hanged later that day on makeshift gallows built onto the front of the jail. After relieving the community of a handful of criminals, the Vigilance Committee of 1856 turned its policing duties back over to the elected officials.

There have been countless assassinations in California. Business transactions go bad, competitors get taken out, and jilted lovers track down their exes and gun them down. Rival criminals target individuals in drive-by shootings almost every day. Assassinations are almost always motivated by personal animus. The common thread tying together the jailbreak assassination of Christian Mutschler and the murder of San Francisco Mayor George Moscone is that in the former incident a handful of people and in the latter incident a deranged individual thought that the world would be a better place without them alive.

Charles Manson disciple Lynette "Squeaky" Fromme is cuffed by U.S. Secret Service agents after she pointed a gun at President Gerald Ford on September 5, 1975, at the state capital building in Sacramento. Fromme didn't know how to properly load and fire the gun. *(Associated Press)*

Gerald Ford, the thirty-eighth president of the United States, had the dubious honor of surviving two assassination attempts in California, only three weeks apart. On September 5, 1975, Lynette "Squeaky" Fromme, a disciple of Charles Manson, pointed a Colt .45 semiautomatic pistol at President Ford while he was in Sacramento. Fromme didn't know how to properly load the pistol, and when she pulled the trigger, nothing happened. Fromme was arrested and sentenced to life in prison for the attempted assassination of a president.

On September 22, 1975, social outcast Sara Jane Moore attempted to shoot President Ford outside of the Saint Francis Hotel in San Francisco. Oliver Sipple, a bystander, grabbed Moore's gun as she raised it to take aim and wrestled her to the ground as she got one shot off. Moore pleaded guilty to attempted assassination of a president and received life in prison.

A stylish woman jumps out of the way as ex-marine Oliver Sipple lunges for Sara Jane Moore seconds after she fired a shot at President Gerald Ford in San Francisco on September 23, 1975. *(Associated Press)*

California justice knows no zip codes. It doesn't acknowledge social standing or appreciate logic. It just does what it has to do, whether it is right or wrong.

Chapter 1

The Sacramento Squatters' Riot

Death Toll: +/- 10

August 14 and 15, 1850, Sacramento—Sacramento County

The hordes of men who flocked to California in an effort to capitalize on the Gold Rush soon learned the price of erecting their tents and shacks on land owned by Captain John Sutter.

The series of events that came to be known as the "Sacramento Squatters' Riot" wasn't a riot at all. It was a shootout between landowners and the landless that grew out of tensions that had been building for years. Sacramento in 1850 was a muddy mess of humanity. In a few short years, the population of non-natives in Sacramento went from a few dozen to over 20,000. The Gold Rush was in full bloom, and thousands of people from all over the world flooded the town, which was the last vestige of so-called "civilization" before the goldfields. Everyday objects were inflated to prices that would be unreasonable even by today's standards. An egg cost one dollar. A shovel cost fifty dollars. Merchants wanted to gouge the miners, and Captain John Sutter was as guilty as anyone. He had been practicing price-gouging on Indians since 1839, and he was eager to fleece a new crop of benefactors.

The heavy influx of people and the shortage of housing meant that most people had no place to stay. Given the nonexistence of anything resembling housing codes, the transients set up their tents and built crude buildings anywhere they chose. Sutter, who owned all the land for miles around, wasn't pleased about the squatters on his property. The squatters, on the other hand, challenged the land grants that the Mexican government had awarded Sutter. The squatters figured that California was now part of the United States, and any deal made with the former Mexican government was null and void. Although Sutter had been financially successful before the Gold Rush, the squatters brought a halt to his new moneymaking strategy involving land sales. He was trying to sell plots of his land, but no developer was interested in buying property with a squatter city occupying it. Although Sutter couldn't effectively prevent the thousands of miners scattered across his vast property from digging for gold, he felt that he could do something about the squatters on his Sacramento property.

Sutter asked Sheriff Joseph McKinney to evict the unlawful residents. The twenty-three-year-old McKinney wasn't enthusiastic about evicting the squatters, as they greatly outnumbered any posse that he could assemble, but he was the only law for miles around and he reluctantly agreed to begin the evictions.

Sheriff McKinney formed a posse and informed the squatters they were to leave immediately. To make sure that the squatters got the point, posse members threw ropes onto several of the flimsy structures and pulled them down before riding off.

The squatters were outraged by the eviction orders. They organized a Settlers' Association headed by Dr. Charles Robinson, who later became governor of Kansas. After several meetings, they elected an additional leader, John P. Maloney. Maloney was a Mexican War veteran, and he became the squatter's military commander.

On August 12, 1850, Dr. Robinson gathered two hundred squatters and their sympathizers at Second and N streets and announced that they would not recognize state authority and would use force to resist any attempts to dislodge them. Sheriff McKinney wisely decided not to make an appearance.

The next day, an arrest warrant was issued for Dr. Robinson, but the doctor was nowhere to be found. Instead, the sheriff arrested several squatters who were quite vocal in their feelings about Dr. Robinson's arrest warrant. The men were put into the prison brig anchored in the Sacramento River.

On August 14, Sheriff McKinney and his men tried to evict some squatters from a house on Second Avenue, but were beaten back by armed men led by Maloney. The squatters, many of them former soldiers, put together a show of force and marched in formation down to L Street and toward the waterfront, attracting the attention of the huddled masses. Maloney was armed with two holstered pistols and a sword. Dr. Robinson came out of hiding and met up with the men. Maloney waved his sword and encouraged his men. Bystanders thought the ragtag soldiers were joking around. Few realized just how serious these men were about the eviction threat.

The squatters' army decided against attacking the heavily guarded prison ship, and about fifty armed protesters marched up J Street. Sacramento's first mayor, Harding Bigelow, intercepted the demonstrators at Fourth and J, accompanied by City Assessor James Woodland, Sheriff McKinney, and his posse. Bigelow read the protestors the riot act, amid jeers and thrown objects. Suddenly and simultaneously, a volley of gunfire erupted on each side, killing squatter Jesse Morgan and an unknown demonstrator outright. City Assessor Woodland was shot in the chest and died shortly after his body crumpled to the ground. James Harper, Dr. Robinson, and two bystanders were wounded. Mayor Bigelow was knocked off his horse when four bullets hit him in the chest. He died in agony a few months later in San Francisco. John Maloney had his horse shot out from under him, but that didn't stop the commander. He ran toward the shooting, his sword slicing the air. The city recorder, Benjamin F. Washington, shot Maloney in the head.

Within moments, both sides panicked and dispersed in every direction. As the smoke cleared, bodies littered a blood-soaked J Street. The dead and the wounded were dragged off, and there was no clear count of exactly how many men died or were wounded in the shootout.

The next day, Sheriff McKinney received word that some of the squatters were hiding in a roadhouse owned by squatter sympathizer William Allan in Brighton. Brighton was a village that existed where today Folsom Avenue dips under U.S. 50, near the State University of California–Sacramento. McKinney formed another posse and rode to the roadhouse.

At the inn, Sheriff McKinney called for everyone inside to come out. Allan answered that his wife was dying and that he'd turn himself in the next morning. But the young and inexperienced McKinney was impatient and irate over the shootout. In total disregard for everyone's safety, he and some of his men charged the inn, burst through the door, and started shooting, killing Allan's son and wounding William Allan. The elder Allan managed to shoot Sheriff McKinney. Sheriff McKinney stumbled back outside toward the rest of the posse and yelled to them, "I'm dead, I'm dead, I'm dead." McKinney then fell face first to the ground, where he died.

The screams, the blood, and the bullets that exploded from a half a dozen guns in her own home was too much for Allan's wife, and she died of shock. Two squatters, George Henshaw and Madison Kelly, also were killed in the shootout.

Although wounded, William Allan escaped from his gunsmoke-filled home and made his way up the American River to the goldfields. Friends and sympathetic strangers sheltered Allan from the law until he was forgotten by the authorities. Subsequently, he remarried, raised a family, and farmed to a ripe old age in Lake County.

The Squatter Riot episode would not be the last time in California history that desperate men killed one another over that most precious of commodities, real estate.

Justice traditionally sides with landed barons, rather than with downtrodden squatters. However, a tide of desperate men can sweep away the dams of justice and flood the land with blood.

Chapter 2

He Said, She Said, They Said; She Was Hanged!

Death Toll: 2

July 5, 1851, Downieville—Sierra County

Emotions and loyalties were powerful forces in the Gold Rush villages of California. In a classic case of contradictory testimony, emotions overpowered reason and compassion, and the early California legal system provided a "suspect" justice.

The rowdy miners who dug the rich gold veins in the hills around Downieville were in the mood to celebrate the Fourth of July in 1851. The seventy-fifth anniversary of America's independence from Great Britain provided ideal justification for the miners to get drunk, fight, and lose some gold dust at the gambling dens and whorehouses.

Downieville consisted of little more than a mud road, lined by bars, hotels, and gaming rooms that straddled both sides of the North Fork of the Yuba River. A rough-hewn log suspension bridge connected the two sides of the Downieville community. The hills surrounding the little town were populated by scores of gold miners and they all trooped into Downieville on July fourth, hooting and hollering.

Mexican War hero and senate candidate Colonel John B. Weller was in Downieville to give a speech, and the post-speech celebration lasted throughout the night and into the fifth of July. Three miners took the celebration to the extreme. Frederick Cannon, Charley Getzler, and another man, identified only as Lawson, partied throughout the night, and

A saloon was always a welcome sight on the California frontier. *(California State Library Photograph Collection)*

at about seven in the morning, the men started banging on doors of the modest hovels of Downieville, attempting to reignite the party.

After beating on a couple of doors, the men started pounding on the door of a house occupied by a couple we know historically only as Jose and Josefa. Jose was a professional gambler and Josefa was his common-law wife. Their last names have been lost to time.

The door couldn't handle the pounding of the miners' fists and fell off its hinges, startling the sleeping couple. The men entered the home and created a disturbance before they put the door back into place.

A couple of hours later, Cannon went into a barbershop near the site of Jose and Josefa's home. Jose entered the barbershop and demanded payment for the broken door. The story goes in two directions at this point, depending upon who's telling it. The first version is that Cannon and Jose stepped outside of the barbershop where Cannon apologized and shook hands with Jose. Josefa, who was visibly angry, approached the men and Cannon also apologized to her. This version certainly seems inexplicable, particularly considering the subsequent events.

The second version, according to another witness, is that Cannon and Jose were arguing in Spanish and Cannon called Josefa a whore, something that she was not. Josefa was enraged and Jose led her back into their home. Cannon and his friend Lawson went to the couple's door and Cannon offered his hand to Josefa in apology. Josefa pulled a large Bowie knife from the fold of her dress and struck Cannon in the heart. Cannon fell gasping into Lawson's arms. He died moments later.

Jose took Josefa to Craycroft's saloon, where his gambler buddies hid her. The hungover miners heard about the stabbing and headed to Craycroft's in huge numbers. The gamblers, being experts in odds making, decided that they were in a no-win situation and released Josefa to the authorities. Since there was no jail in Downieville, they lodged her in a log cabin near where the political speeches had been made the day before.

A miner's court was soon convened and the couple was placed under guard. A judge and prosecutor were picked, a jury was selected, and the couple was provided with two lawyers. Meanwhile, the crowd outside of the cabin had grown to three thousand angry men. An eyewitness described the mob as the "hungriest, craziest, wildest mob" he had ever seen.

An attorney named Thayer stood on the makeshift stage and begged the mob to let the legal courts take care of the matter. He was shouted down, pulled off the stage, and beaten by the horde. Ropes were brought in to keep the crowd in control and the judge had to plead with the men to remember their wives, daughters, and mothers back home. Colonel John Weller, the man running for senator, was still in Downieville, but he wouldn't apply his oratory and leadership skills to prevent a the lynching. Not standing up for Josefa forever haunted his political career.

Cannon's friends, Getzler and Lawson, gave their accounts, as did a twelve-year-old boy who witnessed the stabbing. Jose testified too, stating that Cannon called his common-law wife a whore. Josefa testified on her own behalf, telling the jury that she was afraid that the men had knocked down her door to rape her and she had been frightened by Cannon.

A recess was called at one-thirty in the afternoon so the defense could find more witnesses. Most of the crowd headed for the saloons to tie on another one, but some of the men went to the tent where Cannon's body lay in state. Cannon was a popular guy, and many of his friends were very drunk.

Two more witnesses were called after the recess. A man named McMurray confirmed that he heard Cannon swearing in Spanish. Dr. Cyrus D. Aiken testified that Josefa was pregnant, and therefore she couldn't be hanged. Doctors Chamberlin, Hunter, and Hardy took Josefa to the log cabin to examine her.

The mob went wild, with men shaking their fists at Dr. Aiken and threatening to hang Dr. Aiken along with Josefa. The doctors came back and testified that there was no evidence that Josefa was pregnant. The mob held a vote and elected to kick Dr. Aiken out of town. He wisely left town for a few days immediately afterward to wait until things cooled down.

Alcohol abuse was as common as mustaches in early California. *(California State Library Photograph Collection)*

The jury retired and returned their verdict in short time. They found Josefa guilty of murder and sentenced her to death within two hours. Jose was found not guilty, but he was ordered to leave town within twenty-four hours.

At three forty-five in the afternoon on July 5, 1851, Josefa was led to the suspension bridge over the Yuba River. A crowd of about five hundred stayed to watch the hanging. Over one of the bridge's towers hung a noose that was tied to a beam that worked as a counterweight. A stepladder was set up for the doomed woman to stand upon.

Josefa was emotionless as she climbed the makeshift gallows. She was asked if she had any final words and Josefa exclaimed, "Nothing, but I would do the same again if I were provoked." She asked that her body be turned over to friends for a proper burial. She shook hands with the men standing near her and said, "Adios, señor" to each of them.

Josefa threw her hat to a friend and put the noose around her own neck. She objected to having her hands tied behind her back, but a black hood was placed over her head. At the sound of a pistol shot, the men dumped the beam over the railing and Josefa was flung into the air. She was left hanging by her neck for twenty-two minutes before she was cut down and her body was given to her friends for burial.

Despite valiant efforts—and less than valiant efforts (i.e. Colonel John Weller)—to prevent the execution of a woman, mob emotions prevailed, and Josefa faced her ignominious end with dignity.

Chapter 3

The Greatest Shootout in the West

Death Toll: 13; Wounded: +/- 5

December 19, 1854, North Fork of the American River—El Dorado County

Law enforcement and formal justice were often virtually nonexistent in the wilds of the Gold Rush country. However, even an extensive and powerful law system would certainly have been unable to protect the myriad of miners who scattered themselves across the wilderness mountain areas. In the face of constant violence and ruthless attacks, men were forced to provide their own protection, and to mete out their own justice.

The California Gold Rush of 1849 caused great social disruption around the world. Men left their jobs, families, and friends to try their luck in the goldfields. They came from all walks of life: rich and poor, farmers and city slickers, young and old; they all left their familiar surroundings for flecks of gold. It wasn't just Americans who came to California in the middle of the nineteenth century; men, and a handful of women, came from England, France, Chile, Australia, Ireland, Canada, China, Japan, and Mexico.

Mixing social and economic classes in a lawless wilderness, combined with dozens of different ethnicities, cultures, and languages, created the recipe for a witches' brew of trouble. The heavily forested and lonely trails that crisscrossed the Sierra Nevada mountains were perfect terrain for ambushing and robbing well-equipped prospectors entering the goldfields. It was even more profitable to ambush and rob successful miners carrying sacks of gold back to town. With little resembling law enforcement for hundreds of miles in all directions, travelers had to be alert and aware of their surroundings at all times, as the hills were full of desperate men with foul intentions.

Indentured servitude was often the punishment for early California criminals. *(California State Library Photograph Collection)*

On December 19, 1854, Dr. Bolivar A. Sparks, James C. McDonald, and Captain Jonathan R. Davis, a thirty-eight-year-old veteran of the Mexican War, were trekking on a miner's trail along the North Fork of the American River in El Dorado County. As they hiked through Rocky Canyon, they were bushwhacked by a motley group of bandits. The international bouquet of thugs included a Frenchman, two Americans, two Brits, four Mexicans, and five Australians. All of the men were ruthless killers who had robbed and killed four American miners the day before and six Chinese miners the day before that.

The gang rushed the men with guns ablaze, instantly killing McDonald and fatally wounding Dr. Sparks. Captain Davis, who was known as a skilled marksman and expert fencer, wasted no time in taking down the bandits. He pulled out both of his pistols and blazed away at the outlaws, killing them one by one. He killed seven bandits in as many seconds. Four more outlaws charged Captain Davis, three of them wielding Bowie knives and one a sword. Davis pulled out his Bowie knife and, like the swordsman he was, fought off the four men, killing three and cutting off the nose and several fingers of the fourth man. The last three bandits thought better of taking on Captain Davis and fled into the hills. Despite six bullet holes in the captain's hat, he had only a few minor flesh wounds.

Even though the fight took place deep in the boondocks, a group of miners saw the entire mêlée from a nearby hilltop. Three of them ran to the scene, startling the captain, who quickly went for a dead man's gun to defend himself. The miners quickly explained that they had witnessed the attack and invited him and the gravely wounded Dr. Sparks back to their camp.

In the evening, the entire mining camp of eighteen men and Captain Davis returned to the scene of the crime. Three of the wounded bandits had died. The group searched the bodies and found almost five hundred dollars in gold and silver coins, four ounces of gold dust, and nine gold and silver watches. The noseless, seven-fingered bandit confessed to being party to the bloodbaths of the previous days.

The next morning, the noseless bandit died and was buried with the rest of the dead men, including McDonald. The miners formed a coroner's jury and seventeen miners signed a statement, testifying that they seen the attack and witnessed Captain Davis's defense. Captain Davis then carried Dr. Sparks down from the mountains to his home in Coloma, where he died on December 26.

Being a gentleman from South Carolina, Captain Davis was highly offended when the newspaper accounts of the clash suggested the writers didn't believe the story, as the captain's prodigious defense defied credibility. Captain Davis went to great lengths to prove that he had indeed defended his friends and fought fourteen men, killing eleven of them. The captain's story was officially accepted as truth after a delegation of prominent Placerville citizens hiked up the North Fork of the American River after the snow melted and investigated the crime scene. From then on, Captain Davis was considered a folk hero in Northern California.

Captain Davis's valiant, courageous, and exceptional self-defense in the face of overwhelming odds became legendary in the history of the Gold Rush. On a winter day in December 1854, Captain Davis created his own justice system, and although contemporary journalists temporarily scoffed at his stand, eleven bandits received their punishment.

Chapter 4

Auburn's Darkest Night

Death Toll: 2

February 19, 1856, Auburn—Placer County

Often during the early days of California statehood, prejudice, linked with the momentum of a mob mentality, overruled the best efforts and intentions of the law enforcement and justice systems.

Aaron Bracey was a freed slave who, like thousands of other people from around the world, set out for California during the Gold Rush days. Bracey quickly earned a reputation as a man you didn't want to cross. In 1856, he killed a Chinese man he claimed had burglarized his cabin on his small ranch near Auburn.

On February 18, 1856, Bracey was engaged in a property line dispute with his neighbor James Murphy, an Irish emigrant. No one really knows just what was said or what occurred during the quarrel, but whatever happened made Bracey fly into a rage, grab a pickax, and strike Murphy in the back of the head. Bracey immediately got a doctor and turned himself over to the authorities, explaining to the police that the pickax had accidentally slipped out of his hands. Murphy told the authorities on his deathbed that Bracey had struck him from behind.

Slavery was still legal in America, and many of the miners in the hills were from the Deep South. Murphy was a popular man, and his friends starting lingering around the jail calling for Judge Lynch. Sheriff King and Deputy John Boggs deputized a posse to guard the jail. Fifty more citizens of Auburn were asked be ready to come to the sheriff's aid if they heard the courthouse bells ringing.

Freed slave and accused murderer Aaron Bracey was dragged from the Placer County jail in Auburn and lynched by an angry crowd of miners on February 19, 1856. *(California State Library Photograph Collection)*

At about two-thirty in the morning of February 19, Deputy Boggs spotted a mob approaching the jail. Boggs yelled out to the sheriff and the posse, but by the time they stepped outside of the jail, they were surrounded and disarmed by the mob. One officer managed to ring the courthouse bell, but none of the citizen guards came to the rescue.

As the mob began to break down the jailhouse doors, Sheriff King broke loose and ran to stop them. One of the leaders of the gang stuck a pistol into the sheriff's chest and demanded the key to the jail. Sheriff King grabbed the gun and wrestled with the man, but he was quickly overpowered by the mob.

Aaron Bracey was dragged from his cell and forced to march up the street, as the mob beat him over his head with pick handles and clubs. Father Quinn, a Catholic priest, pleaded with the vigilantes to release the man and let the courts try him, but the frenzied throng was in no mood to listen to a man of the cloth. A handful of vigilantes picked up the priest and threw him over a fence.

Somewhere outside of Auburn, the exact place lost to history, the mob threw a rope over a branch of a pine tree and jerked Bracey into the air. The noose slipped over the terrified man's face as he dangled in the cold night air. The mob lowered Bracey, readjusted the noose and pulled him back up into the air, where he slowly

One of the earliest known photographs of Auburn, California. *(California State Library Photograph Collection)*

strangled to death, as a crowd of two hundred stood by and watched, either too afraid to come to Bracey's rescue or glad to see him get what they felt he had coming.

No doubt there is now a fine home or a shop on the site where Aaron Bracey was lynched. People walk around doing their business or looking at the historic old downtown district, completely unaware of Auburn's darkest night.

> *Auburn had a sheriff and a deputy, a citizen guard force, and a brick-and-mortar jailhouse. However, these were not enough to save Aaron Bracey from the hands of a vigilante mob, despite the noble efforts of Sheriff King. Justice was thwarted and mob violence prevailed.*

Chapter 5

A Serial Lyncher Is Lynched

Death Toll: Unknown (possibly hundreds)

1873, Monterey—Monterey County

Early California justice sometimes displayed a sense of irony and provided its own form of "poetic justice."

Matt Tarpy hated to see crime and disorder. An Irish immigrant, Tarpy came to California during the Gold Rush and settled beside the Pajaro River near Watsonville. A diehard racist, Tarpy seemed to hate everyone, but he had a special hatred for the Californios. To him, they were all thieves, cutthroats, and bandits. Tarpy was a natural leader and he used his organizational skills to bring his version of law and order to the Pajaro Valley and the Monterey Bay area, whether the residents agreed with him or not.

Tarpy first made a name for himself as a vigilante in October 1856, when he captured the notorious outlaw Juan Salazar. Salazar had escaped from the Santa Barbara jail and stolen a herd of horses while making his getaway. He joined up with some of his bandit friends and drove the horses north to the Pajaro River. Salazar and a comrade stayed at Salazar's ex-wife's home, while his gang camped out near the river.

Tarpy and his rancher buddies heard that Salazar was nearby and quickly found the outlaw camp. Entering the cabin, they found Salazar in bed and captured him without a struggle. His friend escaped, as a hail of bullets whizzed past him.

Tarpy and his posse intended to take Salazar to Watsonville, but as they traveled through a dense grove of wild mustard, Salazar allegedly made a break for it. Tarpy and his friends filled him with lead.

At daybreak, Tarpy and his men arrived in Watsonville with Salazar's dead body lying over the back of a horse. A half dozen vaqueros happened to be entering Watsonville at the same time. Tarpy and his company thought that they were Salazar's gang and ordered them to halt. Who fired first is lost to history; however, the Californio cowboys fired some shots, Tarpy's gang fired some shots, and general mayhem commenced.

Everyday people could turn into a murderous lynch mob under stressful circumstances. *(California State Library Photograph Collection)*

The Californios, realizing that it wasn't a good time to visit Watsonville, rode their horses out of town at a full gallop, with Tarpy's gang in hot pursuit. The vaqueros outran the vigilantes, but Tarpy found a blood trail from a wounded horse and his gang followed it to a house a few miles from Watsonville. They apprehended a man with dried blood on his boots into custody and took him back into town.

Tarpy tied the vaquero to a flagpole in the center of town, where he was subsequently identified by Tarpy's group as one of the Californios. The citizens of Watsonville, Anglos and Californios alike, argued about the fate of the man, causing great tension in the dusty town. The prisoner claimed self-defense, and many of the citizens of Watsonville agreed that Tarpy and his pals had fired first. Watsonville had been a settlement for nine years and the residents weren't happy about having a greenhorn, racist Irishman and his irrational followers acting as judge, jury, and executioner in their area.

The next morning, the consensus of the townsfolk was that the prisoner would be handed over to the authorities in San Jose. Tarpy was fervently opposed to the plan, so he freed the prisoner, who ran to his vaquero friends and rode off into the hills. Tarpy and his gang jumped on their horses in pursuit. A running gunfight broke out, but Tarpy's gang managed to capture the poor vaquero again. Instead of taking him to San Jose, they hung him from a tree along the riverbank.

After that incident, Tarpy decided that he was indeed the law of the land, much to the dismay of the people who lived in the area. For the next sixteen years, the residents of Santa Cruz and Monterey counties had to live with the fact that a psychopathic, egomaniacal Irish rancher and a handful of like-minded Anglos dealt out the law according to their own wishes.

There is no way of knowing just how many men Tarpy and his gang lynched, but it is believed that the number included at the very least fifteen Indians and Hispanics. He basically hunted down and shot anyone he thought was a rustler, which to Tarpy meant anyone who wasn't the correct hue of white and didn't speak English.

Tarpy's reign of terror lasted until 1873. The locals, disgusted by the years of Tarpy's racism, tyranny, and brutality, finally had enough of the vigilante after the thug shot a woman named Sarah Nicholson with whom he had a land dispute.

Tarpy took his arrest lightly, figuring that nobody would actually convict him. Imagine his surprise when a crowd of over four hundred Anglos, Californios, and Hispanics broke into the Monterey jail in the middle of the night and took him captive. They took him three miles out of town in a wagon and hung him from a tree. A Californio placed the noose around Tarpy's neck before they jerked him up into the damp ocean air.

Although Matt Tarpy never received a trial and became the victim of vigilante justice, it appears obvious that he met his just desserts. The patience of an oppressed citizenry cannot be strained indefinitely, and in this case punishment was meted out, not for a single crime, but for the actions of a longtime reign of terror.

Chapter 6

The Lynching of an Uninvited Wedding Guest

Death Toll: 2

December 20 and December 22, 1875,
Sanel and Hopland—Mendocino County

Social events in nineteenth-century California were at a premium. When these events were forestalled or interrupted by violent, antisocial interlopers, vigilante justice was quick to ensue.

During the frontier days in California, a wedding was one of the biggest events that a muddy little town like Sanel could experience. In the last quarter of 1875, the first generation of California-born Caucasian females were reaching marrying ages. Thomas Flanagan and Mary Pina tied the knot on December 20, 1875, and everyone from miles around attended the wedding. The Christmas season was in high gear, and the harvest-weary farmers were ready to kick back and have a good time. The Flanagan/Pina wedding was a good excuse to dress up and visit with friends and neighbors, and maybe even get a bit of Christmas shopping done between the service and the reception.

The reception dance was held at Pina's aunt's home, where the merrymakers danced to a band into the early morning hours. Well into the celebration, William Granjean stood up on a table to cheer on the dancing guests. Outside the house, lurking in the shadows, was a man named Jose Antonio Ygarra. Ygarra was out on bail awaiting trial for horse theft, and Granjean was to be the main witness against him. He could see Granjean standing on the table with his back to a window, waving his arms and doing a jig. Ygarra pulled out his pistol, walked towards the window, and shot Granjean in the back of the head. Then, Jose Ygarra ran away as fast as he could run.

The report of the pistol and a blood-spouting corpse put an end to the party. Granjean was dead before he hit the floor; the bullet had pierced his skull, gone through his brain, and smashed against the inside of his frontal bones. He was shot at such close range that there were powder burns on the outside windowpane.

Wedding guest Weaver Andrews told the shocked gathering that he had encountered Jose Antonio Ygarra outside of the house and that Ygarra had asked him if Granjean was attending the reception. Ygarra was tracked down and arrested two days later, on December 22. Nearly every man and boy in the valley turned out for the inquiry hearing, over which Justice Dooly of Sanel presided. Most of the men were armed and agitated, and there were whispers of a lynching.

At six in the evening, a group of twenty men took the prisoner from the courtroom and led him off into the darkness. When the men returned, they reported that the prisoner had escaped.

The next morning Ygarra's corpse was found hanging from a live oak tree a few miles down the road outside of Hopland, near the Russian River. A few years later, there would be other questionable cases of California justice in Mendocino County.

Jose Antonio Ygarra eliminated the witness who could put him away, but in doing so, he created an overwhelming social angst. As a result, Jose missed the party and attended the hangman's ball instead.

Chapter 7

A Cold Welcome to Santa Cruz

Death Toll: 3

May 3, 1877, Santa Cruz—Santa Cruz County

Most new immigrants to California had little realization of the perils that lurked on the poorly policed streets of the explosively growing towns. Having come from Eastern states that provided established and efficient law enforcement protection, these innocents could not possibly anticipate the lethal dangers they faced.

Henry de Forrest was excited about his new life in California. The sixty-two-year-old carpenter had left his wife and young children in Maine while he looked for opportunities in the Golden State. He quickly found employment in his trade at the Powder Mill wharf operation in Santa Cruz, and he was excited about sending for his family. He found life very good in Santa Cruz. Its beautiful location on the sea, good weather, and the forest-covered mountains were sure to please his family. Plus, there was plenty of work for a carpenter. They would all soon start a new life in California.

April 29, 1877, was a beautiful Saturday evening and de Forrest was enjoying a walk through the small city, taking in the fresh spring air. Maybe he stopped for a drink at one of the many saloons or got a bite to eat. As he was walking on River Street near the present Farmers Exchange, ex-cons Francisco Arias and Jose Chamales accosted the elderly carpenter. Arias shot de Forrest in the chest with a large-caliber revolver, and the two men dragged him fifty feet off the street into the brush , where they went through his pockets for money. Arias and Chamales then went to a saloon called the Aptos Circus and spent the dead man's money, just as if they had earned it honestly.

In the morning, a passerby discovered de Forrest's lifeless body and ran for the police. The sheriff had barely started his investigation when a Californio came forward and told him about a frightening encounter that he had had the night before. Before Arias and Chamales attacked de Forrest, the bandits stopped the Californio at the same spot where de Forrest was murdered and robbed. The man was from a Native American village located a mile north of Santa Cruz and the bandits recognized him. They decided not to rob him.

Francisco Arias had murdered before. He had killed a sheepherder and was sent to San Quentin. Most sheepherders in the early history of California were either Mexican or Native American, which is probably why Arias didn't get the death pentalty—even in the courtroom, California justice was not applied equally. San Quentin was like a home away from home for Arias, as he had served time there for robbery before the murder of the sheepherder.

At twenty-one years of age, Jose Chamales was already a veteran of the San Quentin prison. Robbery was second nature to the Santa Cruz native and he had previously paid the price for his crimes.

Armed with the information provided by the Californio who had been spared from robbery by Arias and Chamales, the sheriff went to visit Chamales' mother, who evidently didn't approve of her son's lifestyle. She implied that her son was probably involved with the crime, and she may have even revealed where he might be hiding. A few days later, the sheriff's deputies found Chamales ensconced in Watsonville and Arias camped out with two women near the road to San Juan Bautista.

Chamales told the deputies that Arias had pulled the trigger and had only given him $2.50 as his cut, whereas Arias' take was $17.50. Chamales thought that he had should have received more of the split. However, both men were in the Santa Cruz jail by Tuesday.

The next night, May 3, 1877, somewhere between forty and three hundred masked men descended on the jail and easily convinced the two guards to release the bandits into their care. The frightened criminals were marched to the Water Street bridge over the San Lorenzo River, and nooses were placed around their necks. They were given a shot of whiskey and were allowed to say a few last words. What they said was never written down, except it was noted that they spoke in Spanish. They were then hoisted up and left hanging until they were discovered the next morning. When they were cut down in mid-morning, the ropes were divided into foot-long sections and given away as souvenirs.

On the night of May 3, 1877, as they hovered above their destines on the Water Street bridge, Arias and Chamales certainly would have preferred a stay in their old digs at San Quentin.

Chapter 8

False Friends in Germantown

Death Toll: 1

May 5, 1878, Germantown/Artois—Colusa County

In the early days of California statehood, friendships and alliances could be tenuous, particularly among those who harbored secrets and who often operated beneath the law. In fact, friendships were often illusory, and sometimes lethal.

Not much is known about Christian Mutschler, but what is known indicates that he wasn't a very intelligent man. The Germantown blacksmith certainly made poor choices in his friends.

On May 5, 1878, Mutschler (also spelled Mutchler), along with two of his buddies, John Kelley and Henry Holmes, had words with a saloonkeeper named Hageman. Mutschler, who was mentally the slowest member of the group and was suspected to have been an arsonist, was persuaded by Kelley and Holmes—along with W. Hagaman, F. Todt, Charles Hansen, and Carl Regensberger—to collect a sack of wood shavings to use to set a fire in Hageman's saloon. They figured they'd all get a good laugh by stinking up the place.

Inside the saloon, Mutschler's buddies gave him the signal to torch the shavings. As he began to ignite the bag, a couple of no-nonsense cowboys pulled out their pistols and shot Mutschler in the leg, preventing the intended conflagration.

Brought before Germantown's justice of the peace, named in the press only as Boardman, Mutschler was charged with arson. No charges were brought against the cowboys, its being perfectly legal in California to shoot someone committing a prank in a drinking establishment. But since no one would testify against Mutschler, Justice Boardman released him.

Mutschler may have been stupid, but he was smart enough to know that it was a good time to leave Germantown. Suffering under the hot spring sun, the blacksmith started limping in the direction of Orland. He had to walk because all of the stage drivers leaving Germantown had been instructed not to give him a ride. Mutschler was being set up.

Justice in California functioned in baffling ways throughout the early days of California statehood, and this was particularly true in 1878. For some reason, Mutschler's friend, John Kelley, swore out a warrant on Mutschler for having threated his life. A deputy was sent up the road toward Orland to apprehend the wounded and hapless Mutschler. Mutschler was corralled and placed under arrest until he could make his thousand-dollar bond, which was quite impossible for a humble blacksmith.

Mutschler was put into the protective custody of Constable William McLane, who also owned a Germantown saloon. Since Germantown had no jail, McLane housed the blacksmith in his bar for the night. It proved a bad idea, because sometime during the night, a group of twelve to fourteen masked men broke down the door to McLane's saloon. They grabbed Mutschler, took him some 250 to 300 yards out of town and shot him to death.

Mutschler's friends, Holmes, Kelley, Hansen, Regensberger, and a man identified only as R. Radcliff, were all arrested in the investigation. Constable McLane apparently wasn't suspected of dereliction of duty or wrongdoing. Hagaman, Todt, and a man named Oscar Scholtz were taken to Willows for examination, where they were subsequently held on $10,000 bail, which they immediately paid.

According to the testimony of Constable McLane, the masked men had broken down the door to his saloon and pointed their pistols at the officer. They took Mutschler away and ten minutes later, McLane heard the fatal shots.

John Kelley testified that he was asleep when the "jailbreak" occurred. Under oath, Kelley stated that although there was never any difficulty between him and the victim, Mutschler had on one occasion made direct threats against Kelley's life if he revealed certain secrets that they shared.

Radcliff, Regensberger, Holmes, Kelley, and Hansen were brought before Judge A. Caraloff at Willows, and after four days of examination, they were all charged with murder. The men hired the attorneys A. L. Hart of Colusa and General Lewis of Tehama and pled not guilty. The men were released to the custody of the sheriff of Colusa County but were later released by Judge Keyser on an $8,000 bail.

Mutschler's brother Ludwig hired R. B. Hall, a private detective from San Francisco, to investigate the murder and found evidence that the men had threatened Mutschler's life and had been overheard doing so. The men had also tried to enlist several other Germantown men to join their party.

On August 31, 1878, the *Colusa Sun* reported, "These cases are going to cost the county an immense amount of money at best, and when we see it needlessly squandered, we feel that it is time to put in a protest." Legal fees submitted by detective Hall prodded the *Sun* to add that "if smart San Francisco detectives must do anything, let them hunt up evidence, and not undertake to put the county to so much expense for nothing."

California governor William Irwin offered a $500 reward for the arrest and conviction of any of the assassins, but no one was ever awarded the money.

The trial of "People vs. John Kelley, H. P. Holmes, Carl Regensberger, R. Radcliff, and C. Hansen" was initially set for September 18, but it was later postponed until December 14, 1878. On December 7, the district court dropped the charges against all parties indicted for the killing of Mutschler—"for the reason that important witnesses for the people cannot be found."

Whether because of his mental handicap or his penchant for starting fires, Mutschler obviously wasn't a very popular person in Germantown. Perhaps he was murdered because he knew something that he wasn't supposed to know, but this fact can never be proven. Being a blacksmith, Mutschler may have been hired to make incriminating paraphernalia for outlaws, like burglary tools and irons to change brands. The townspeople may have just been tired of his lighting fires in the dry Sacramento Valley, where an entire town could turn into ashes in minutes.

Postscript: During World War I, there were very strong anti-German feelings throughout many parts of the country and many German-named towns across America were renamed. The U.S. Post Office discontinued the local Germantown name and adopted the name of Artois on May 21, 1918.

> *While the word "justice" does not appear to apply to the case of Christian Mutschler, et al., Mutschler's lack of probity and his poor choice of comrades led him irrevocably to his fate. While Mutschler's "friends" escaped punishment for his murder, it is likely they spent their subsequent days "looking over their own shoulders."*

Chapter 9

The Lynching of
Indian Charlie

Death Toll: 1

May 6, 1878, Walker Valley—Mendocino County

Early California justice seldom extended its dubious protection to Native Americans. And, vigilante justice was often motivated by bias and hatred. Given the attitudes in Mendocino County following the Modoc War, any Native American suspected of a crime, particularly against a white settler, could expect no leniency or compassion.

Mendocino County was still a very wild place in the mid-1870s. The Modoc War had just ended in 1873, and feelings still ran high against the Native Americans. As much as many of the American emigrants wanted to do so, they just couldn't kill every single Native American.

It was a seasonable, sunny day on May 6, 1878, when an unnamed female rode her horse to visit a friend and have dinner in Walker Valley. A well-known Native American named Charlie Modoc was sharpening his large knife in the yard of the lady's friend. No one thought anything about it, as Indian Charlie wasn't thought of as a danger to white people.

After dinner, the unnamed lady mounted her horse and headed home. Not far down the road, Indian Charlie accosted her, pulling her off her horse, and dragging her into the brush. During the struggle, Charlie slashed her several times with his knife. The woman thought quickly and screamed, "That man will kill you." Charlie looked up, saw a man who just happened to be passing by, and then fled the scene, leaving the bloody and beaten woman in the brush. The woman crawled to the road, where a passing buggy gave her a lift back to her friend's house.

A party of angry men formed and went in search of Indian Charlie, and the posse found him about eight in the evening. They strung him up by the neck from a tree and then, to make sure that he was dead, shot his body to pieces.

"California Justice" was carried out, and there was one less Indian for the white settlers to worry about. It is likely that Indian Charlie received what was coming to him. However, even had his guilt been less obvious, he would certainly have spent his final moments staring at one noose or another.

Chapter 10

The Odd Fellows Serve Rough Justice on a Southerner

Death Toll: 2

May 9 through June 9, 1878, Windsor and Santa Rosa—Sonoma County

While mob justice in early California was certainly not officially condoned, it was often difficult to circumvent. An angry mob was a frightening, dangerous thing, and the authorities could be forgiven for allowing discretion to become the better part of valor.

Charles Henley was an ornery cuss. The fifty-seven-year-old farmer had taken some guff from his neighbors for allowing his hogs to run wild on his land—and, they also often strayed onto the property of his neighbors. Henley and his wife had lived on their land north of Windsor in Sonoma County since the late 1860s. Originally from Missouri, Henley supported the Confederacy during the Civil War, which didn't make him very popular in Sonoma County after the war was over.

On May 9, 1876, word was passed on to Henley that some of his stray hogs had been rounded up and corralled by his neighbor, James Rowland. The hotheaded Henley grabbed his shotgun and went to Rowland's ranch.

Finding nobody about on the Rowland property, Henley was in the process of releasing his hogs when Rowland came running from his barn, cursing Henley as he ran toward the corral. Henley responded by blasting holes in Rowland's head with his shotgun. Henley then went home to his wife and told her that he couldn't find the hogs.

Later that evening, Henley, obviously regretting the murder of his neighbor, rode over to Robert Greening's ranch to seek advice on how to handle the situation. Knowing that Greening's hired hand Bill Goodman was a member of the Odd Fellows, as had been James Rowland, he asked Greening not to say anything about their discussion to his hired hand. But Goodman was a cagey cowboy and he was listening in on the men's conversation.

Henley then rode into Windsor and turned himself in to the authorities.

Back at the Rowland ranch, hired hand Joe Dennigan arrived at the ranch around midnight and found Rowland's body in the corral. The farm animals had eaten the damaged parts of the rancher, mutilating him almost beyond recognition. Dennigan rode to a neighbor's ranch and told John Hopper what he had seen.

On May 10, Coroner Kelly Tighe held an inquest, with twelve men in attendance. They decided immediately that Henley had killed Rowland. The remains of Rowland's body were gathered and he was buried according to the Odd Fellows' rites.

A preliminary examination was to be held on May 20 in Santa Rosa before Justice James H. McGee, but Henley's attorneys waived examination until the grand jury was dismissed. Meanwhile, Henley remained in jail.

In the early morning hours of June 9, groups of men began arriving in Santa Rosa. They split into squads and posted themselves in key downtown intersections, detaining anyone who wandered in the area, even policemen.

A squad went to the home of jailer Sylvester H. Wilson and roused him and his family from their beds. The mob told Wilson that they were going to take justice into their own hands and punish Henley for Rowland's murder, and they needed Wilson to go to the jail and hand over the keys to them. They left a group of men to guard his family so they couldn't raise an alarm. Wilson did what he was told to do.

The mob unlocked the jail cell, grabbed Henley, gagged and bound him, and carried him out the door. Another group of men took Wilson and R. Dryer, a night watchman they had captured, and loaded them into a wagon. They drove the men to the outskirts of Santa Rosa and released them. On their way back to town, they met the rest of the lynch mob as they were leaving town.

By the time Dryer and Wilson made it back to the jail, word of the lynching had traveled throughout the town. City Marshal Jim M. White, Dryer, Wilson, Frank Carillo, and freed hostage Officer Fuller went back to the country area where Dryer and Wilson had been released and found Henley hanging by his neck from a tree.

The public was outraged that Santa Rosa's finest would fold so easily, shucking their duties as protectors of the public and allowing armed men to seize a county prisoner for execution. Many people believed that Santa Rosa's police force was in cahoots with the lynch mob. Officers Fuller, Wilson, and Dyer took most of the heat, but in the end they were not punished for having avoided their duty as peace officers. A reward of two thousand dollars was offered for the conviction of any members of the lynch mob, but it was never collected. Nobody knows what happened to Henley's body after the authorities cut him down, and there is no record as to what happened to Henley's wife or his estate.

Charles Henley murdered John Rowland in cold blood. While he obviously deserved due process of law, his temperament and his Southern sympathies weighed heavily against him, and the passions of the fraternal, but not always so benevolent, order of the Odd Fellows held sway.

Chapter 11

A Hard Road into Bakersfield

Death Toll: 9

May 28, 1879, Bakersfield—Kern County

Justice was thwarted in the following case of the Yoakum brothers, as in one trial, they were exonerated, and in another, they were convicted on the basis of highly partial testimony, testimony provided by the victims' relatives and friends. However, based upon exasperation at the lengthy and multiple trial proceedings, and upon the dubious degree of impartiality provided by the judge, some citizens of Bakersfield took the law into their own hands. They drew their own verdict and administered a much quicker form of "justice" than the courts were providing.

The city of Bakersfield is situated at the southern end of the San Joaquin Valley on the Kern River, and it gained a well-deserved reputation as a tough town almost from its founding. Maybe it's the heat.

Bakersfield was settled in 1858, and it was named after an early settler, Colonel Thomas Baker. Colonel Baker ran a sort of campground for immigrants who were moving from southern California looking for a place to settle. By 1871, the settlement had a telegraph office, two stores, a newspaper, two boarding houses, one doctor, a wagon shop, a harness shop, one attorney, a saloon, and fifty students who attended a one-room school. Bakersfield quickly became the center of agriculture and industry for the region.

Five Californios were charged with the ever-popular crime of rustling on December 22, 1877, in Kern County. Whether they were guilty or not, Bessena Ruiz, Fermin Eldeo, Miguel Elias, Francisco Ensinas, and Anthony Maron were all strung up together in one of the biggest lynchings in California history. Nobody was ever charged with the murders.

Bill and Tom Yoakum were successful miners and businessmen in the area. Their land was located about twenty-five miles northeast of Bakersfield and the property included the Long Tom, the New Years Gift, and the Long Hank mines. The brothers also ran a general store, a blacksmith shop, and a mill. They employed thirty miners at their various excavations. The brothers defended their property against claim jumpers and thieves and thought nothing of suing anyone who challenged their right to their lands. Bill Yoakum even ran for sheriff once, although he lost the election.

Don Pedro Bar is one of many towns in California that no longer exist. This photo was taken in 1856. *(California State Library Photograph Collection)*

The Yoakum brothers were not to be messed with, and their success in the mines and the courts angered many citizens of Kern County. Hamilton J. "Tug" Tucker and his partners, Johnson, Bronough, and Webb, were involved in a long-running lawsuit over the Long Tom mine. The lawsuit became convoluted, and the Yoakums filed a court case against Tucker, Johnson, Bronough, and Webb. Little is known about the relationship that Tug Tucker and William Johnson had with their partners. But we can be reasonably sure that the extended lawsuit against the Yoakums drained the capital of both parties.

On April 13, 1879, Tucker and Johnson were driving their wagons along the road approximately a half mile from the Long Tom mine. They were returning from Granite Station, where the thirty-year-old Tug had established his family home. Johnson and Tucker's sister, known only as Mrs. Burdett, were in the front wagon, with Tucker, his wife Harriet, and their two children in the second wagon, when two shots rang out from a rock outcropping on the hillside. Tucker was shot through the heart and died instantly. Johnson was also hit, and he died almost as quickly. People living nearby heard the commotion and came to their aid, but there was nothing they could do. Also, the men had been shot from a distance that was too far for anyone to have seen their assailants.

Harriet Tucker and her sister-in-law attended the coroner's inquest the next day in Bakersfield. Both women were dressed in black. Mrs. Burdett's face was badly bruised from her fall from the wagon. The Yoakums' attorney, a Mr. Gregg, asked Judge Colby to clear the courtroom for the inquest, and the judge agreed. This riled the dead men's friends, and as they stood outside the courthouse, they conjured up explanations as to why the courtroom had been cleared. A few hours later, Coroner A. A. Mix released the results of the inquest. Sheriff W. R. Bower's investigation showed that the shots came from a large boulder with a natural hole in it that served as a gunport for the sniper. The boulder was located two hundred and fifty yards from where the men were shot. The inquest dubiously concluded that the men were probably shot by the Yoakum brothers. Bill and Tom Yoakum were charged with murder, solely because of their ongoing lawsuit and the location of the shooting.

Completely disregarded by the inquest panel was the fact that Tucker and Johnson had successfully sent a miner to prison for stealing their gold. The miner had sworn revenge, and he had been seen around Kern County at the time of the ambush.

The Yoakums' attorney asked for a change of venue for the trial, but Judge Philip Colby refused, although, ironically, before Colby had become a judge, he had represented William Yoakum in an unsuccessful lawsuit against a man named Thomas Baker. Although Bill and Tom Yoakum had huge investments in the area and a payroll to meet, they were detained in the Bakersfield jail while awaiting trial.

The Bakersfield newspapers stirred up passions with stirring editorials that suggested the good citizens of Kern County take the law into their own hands and become the judge, jury, and executioner.

Bill Yoakum's trial started on January 13, 1879. Yoakum was represented by three law firms. The attorneys again requested a change of venue, supported by a document signed by three outstanding Bakersfield citizens. The judge once again refused the request. Harriet Tucker testified first and added new details about the shooting. She now remembered that she recognized Tom and Bill Yoakum running from the ambush site. It was hard to believe that in the commotion, with her husband shot dead while sitting next to her, with their children on their laps and frightened horses pulling their wagon, she had possessed the mindset to look up to see who was shooting at them.

Tucker's sister, Mrs. Burdett, testified that she saw a Yoakum running up the canyon just after the shooting, carrying a rifle. Bill Yoakum's only alibi came from his wife Callie, who told the jury that Bill was home that day, taking care of their sick child while she did the washing.

The jury deliberated for only a few minutes before they came back with a not guilty verdict. Sheriff Bowers had to protect Bill Yoakum from the crowd, which was hell-bent for blood, albeit not justice. Bill still had to face another trial on February 13 for the murder of Johnson. The brothers were pallid and baggy-eyed from their long imprisonment while awaiting trial and they had almost had enough. However, they hired additional attorneys from San Francisco for the next trial. The Bakersfield newspapers spread hate via editorials insinuating that the Yoakums had bought off Judge Colby, completely omitting that Yoakum was found not guilty by a jury of his peers and not the judge.

The Johnson murder trial lasted ten days. Even though Bill had been found not guilty in the first trial, he was found guilty of shooting Johnson. The jury heard the same witnesses and evidence as in the first trial. Yoakum's attorneys immediately filed for a stay of sentencing so that they could appeal the verdict.

Any subsequent appeal trial was scheduled to be moved away from Bakersfield. Unfortunately, the Yoakums were still being held in the Bakersfield jail.

At half past midnight on the morning of May 28, 1879, a mob broke down the door of the jail and grabbed guards George Reed and William H. Coons. They took the keys from the jailers and went looking for the Yoakums. Sheriff Bower and a friend were nearby, but they were stopped by the mob and brazenly held at gunpoint.

The Yoakum brothers were in their cells when the lynch mob entered. Bill, who was in leg irons because he wasn't a model prisoner, fought his attackers like a wildcat, until someone shot him in the chest. They then hung him by the neck in his cell. Tom was murdered the same way.

The jailers were released and they ran for their lives into the night. A few hours after the mob left, the frightened guards entered the jail and found the Yoakums beaten, lynched, and shot.

Even though only a handful of the mob wore masks, and the sheriff and jailers all saw who was involved, the coroner concluded that "unknown persons" had lynched the Yoakums.

> *Evidently, the supporters of the victims had their own opinions as to the events that had led to the ambush murder of Tucker and Johnson. When "justice" flows from the barrel of a rifle, the "law" sometimes becomes irrelevant.*

Chapter 12

The Citizens of Little Lake Strike Back

Death Toll: 3

September 4, 1879, Little Lake—Mendocino County

The Frost family was a blight on the small community of Little Lake. Its outrageous and deadly antics finally wore out the terrified citizens of the village, and a terrible, albeit justified, punishment was meted out to Elijah Frost and his nasty cohorts.

The rough and tumble cities and mining towns weren't the only places where vigilante justice raised its ugly head. Trouble also had a way of brewing in idyllic places like Little Lake in Mendocino County. In 1879, the little hamlet, which is now a neighborhood of Ukiah, was taken over by Elijah Frost, Abijah Gibson, and Thomas McCracken. These constantly drunken ruffians committed petty larcenies and generally made life unpleasant for the townsfolk.

The group's leader was Elijah Frost, a member of the deadly Frost clan that was involved in a longtime Mendocino County feud with the equally homicidal Coates family. Elijah's father, Elisha, had been murdered on October 16, 1867, in the infamous "Little Lake Election Day Shootout."

Prior to that shootout, the Frost clan arrived in Northern California from Missouri around 1858. Working as sheepherders and hog raisers, the always well-armed family was known as a bunch of troublemaking thugs. Their idea of a fun night out was getting roaring drunk and shooting up a Native American ranchero. The Confederate-supporting Frost family became even more obnoxious during the Civil War.

The Coates family arrived in Mendocino County at about the same time as did the Frost clan. The Coateses were from Pennsylvania and they supported the Union. Bad blood flowed between the families, and there were frequent beatings and public arguments, usually over politics. It all came to a head in one of the bloodiest shootouts in California history.

October 16, 1867, was an election day and the citizens of Mendocino County meandered into Little Lake to vote, have a drink, and do a little socializing. It was a warm day and Little Lake was crowded with families.

Members of the Frost family saw the Coates family pull up in a big farm wagon loaded with relatives. Elisha, Martin, and Isom Frost picked a fight with the Coateses that ended in a shootout that killed Albert, Henry, Thomas, Abraham, and Wesley Coates. Abner Coates shot Elisha Frost in the chest with a double-barreled shotgun. Three other participants were seriously wounded.

As a result of the shootout, Elijah Frost was left fatherless at age seventeen. Three years later, Elijah's mother Amanda died. Although he twenty-one years old, the wild Elijah and his three brothers were left in the care of their brother in-law, James McKindley, who soon threw up his hands in frustration.

Elijah was apprehended a couple of times with stolen produce and livestock, but charges were dropped due to lack of evidence. In September 1875, Elijah, along with his wife Mary and fourteen-year-old brother Jimmy, started on a horse-stealing excursion, traveling around northern California, pilfering horses whenever it was convenient.

They made the mistake of stealing sixteen horses from a Shasta County rancher named Joseph Brock. Brock wasn't the type to let anyone get away with stealing his livestock. Teaming up with Tehama County Deputy Sheriff O. A. Lovett and Butte County Sheriff S. L. Daniels, the men tracked down the rustlers, finally catching up with them a few miles from Oroville. Mary and Jimmy were released, but Elijah was sentenced to four years in San Quentin.

The people of Little Lake were taken aback when Elijah was released after serving only thirty-two months of his sentence. Prison had only intensified his obnoxious behavior. He teamed up with fellow thugs Abijah Gibson and Thomas McCracken, and the trio was off and running, committing petty thievery, break-ins, and senseless vandalism, and making a general nuisance of themselves to the people of Little Lake. The men enjoyed hooting and hollering and firing their pistols in the streets of the town. People became afraid to go out on the streets in fear that the drunken gang would harass them, beat them up, or worse.

The hooligans killed an entire flock of geese and tied their heads to the rails of a fence. When a man implied that the ruffians were responsible, his barn was burnt down.

The final straw came when the men were caught stealing a set of harnesses in September 1879. The shackled prisoners were taken to the town of Willits and jailed at Brown's Hotel. While waiting for their September 4 preliminary hearing, the gang threatened revenge against anyone who testified against them.

The townspeople were terrified of what would happen if the men were released or escaped. They formed a vigilante committee to take care of the problem, and during the early morning hours of September 4, they made their move.

Little Lake citizens wanted to send a clear message to other ruffians and drifters who thought they could terrorize the town with impunity. The determined crowd took the three men (two were handcuffed together) to the customary site of summary execution, a local bridge.

Then, during a solemn moment, the men were pushed off the bridge, their necks snapping as a rope borrowed from a local farmer became taut above their weight. According to the local *Dispatch Democrat*, "During the proceedings not a word was uttered."

Following the hasty execution, the bodies of the condemned men dangled from the bridge until Thursday afternoon. News of the lynching traveled quickly through the string of valley towns in northern California.

Immediately upon hearing of the incident, County Coroner Dozier and District Attorney Haile hastened from Ukiah City, the county seat, and held an inquiry at the scene. They interviewed the two jail guards, both of whom had been "compelled" to act as they had during the incident, and they could not identify a single man in the vigilante posse. Masks, the guards testified, obscured identification, though they did admit that none of the men appeared to be young.

Locals praised the lynching for the promise of peace the incident brought with it. According to the local press, "the way in which the good people of

Little Lake have been harassed and intimidated may to some degree at least palliate for the decided step, and will probably forever suppress the riotous actions which at times annoy the place. Some think that more blood will be spilled, but we believe that this will intimidate the gang…"

Sometimes, in early California, community justice, while acting beyond the normal limits of legality, answered the demands of self-preservation and brought a return of social order. The longtime deprivations of the Frost family severely violated the accepted guidelines of social decorum, and Elijah Frost and his cohorts suffered a terrible vengeance.

Chapter 13

The Biggest Coward in Butte County

Death Toll: 2

August 7 and August 8, 1881, Butte County

Bullies and misfits usually end up getting what's coming to them, and when it happens, "poetic justice" has certainly prevailed.

By the early 1880s, Chico was a bustling city of dirt streets and wooden buildings, a citadel of commerce at the northern edge of the Sacramento Valley. Jack Crum was a pioneer in the area and was well known and well liked by the citizens of Butte County.

Crum had once been a rich farmer who owned one of the most beautiful spreads in the Sacramento Valley. It included farmland, orchards, forests, and a picturesque creek that wandered past his large two-story home. Crum had many friends in northern California, and his home was a popular stopping-off place for travelers on the road down the valley.

Eventually, silt and mining waste from the Cherokee hydraulic mine poured down the creek and ruined Crum's property. The mining company paid off a judge or politician and so only had to reimburse Crum pennies on the dollar for the damage to his spread, leaving the old pioneer a financially broken man. Crum left his beloved property and moved into Chico.

Tom Noacks was a big, double-fisted bully who liked to punch out oxen, just like Mongo in the Mel Brooks' comedy *Blazing Saddles*. On August 7, 1881, the moronic Noacks got into a quarrel with the feeble, tottering Crum. Noacks knocked Crum down with his fists and then stomped him to death with his heavy boots.

Oroville's Union House Hotel as it looked when Tom Noacks was taken from the Oroville jail and lynched by an unknown group of men. *(California State Library Photograph Collection)*

Noacks was quickly arrested and jailed, but as word spread that the youthful town bully had killed the old and feeble pioneer, the citizens of the northern Sacramento Valley town started talking about a necktie party. The police soon got word about the general public's feelings about Crum's murder and they knew that, in addition to being a man with many friends, Crum was also a Mason. The police secretly spirited Noacks to the more secure county jail in Oroville.

Nothing is a secret for long in a small town. Friends of Crum gathered quickly and quietly in preparation for Noacks' lynching. In the light of the late summer moonlight, men could be seen carrying axes, ropes, and sledgehammers all over the environs of Chico. Butte County sheriff Sprague was in Chico, but by the time he became aware of the plot, there was little he could do. He sent a telegram to Oroville to warn the jailers about the advancing mob. Mysteriously, the sheriff's cable was never received.

The friends of Jack Crum quietly entered Oroville, posting men strategically to prevent any word from getting out to potential rescuers. A group of men walked to the jail and knocked on the door, where they informed the jailers that they had a prisoner from the town of Biggs. When the iron door was opened, the mob rushed into the jail, overpowering the startled jailers.

Big Tom Noacks cried for mercy and let out pitiful yells as the lynch mob approached his jail cell. The sledgehammers made quick work of Noacks' cell door and in no time he was dragged from the jail and thrown into a waiting wagon. The mob rode in procession to Crum's old ranch, where a noose was thrown over an old cottonwood tree, and Noacks danced the hangman's jig. It was reported that Noacks bellowed like a calf from the time he left the jail until the noose cut off his wind.

Noacks was a big, intimidating man in life, but there was never a bigger coward in Butte County who died with his boots on.

Jack Crum suffered calamity during his life, and his murder, at the hands of a brazen bully, was an obscenity. While morally and legally reprehensible, the lynching of Tom Noacks, sniveling coward that he proved to be, brought the curtain down on an early California Greek tragedy.

Chapter 14

Violated Trust, Trussed Up

Death Toll: 3

April 7 and July 10, 1887, St. John—Glenn County
and Colusa—Colusa County

Mob mentality draws its own verdict, based upon the passions of the moment. When a jury verdict and a judge-mandated sentence conflicts with the desires of an enraged mob, the mob's verdict generally prevails.

Seventeen-year-old Hong Di was employed as a houseboy for the Joseph Billiou family. Billiou owned a large ranch near Saint John in what is now Glenn County, and he lived there with his Irish-born wife Julie and their four children. Little is known about how the family treated the teen-aged houseboy from China, but it couldn't have been well, because on April 7, 1887, as supper was being served, Di walked into the Billious' dining room with a loaded Colt revolver and shot the Billiou family-friend William H. Weaver in the shoulder. The young man then turned and shot Mrs. Billiou square in the heart, killing her instantly.

Di next fired a shot at daughter Annie, barely missing her. Annie ran out of the room as Di fired at her again. Di must have had a lot of animosity toward Annie because he chased her throughout the house, shooting at the girl all the while. At one point, Annie peeked around a door only to be narrowly missed by a bullet fired by Di. As shots continued to ring out, daughter Maude dove out of an open window and ran a mile and a half to St. John for help. Di, his pistol empty, ran to the nearby Sacramento River and disappeared into the thick vegetation that grew along its banks.

Posses were formed, and scores of Chinese males in northern California were questioned and harassed. Fear spread through the Chinese communities and mining camps that an alcohol-fueled posse would mistake one of them for Di. That is what exactly happened in nearby Butte County on April 10.

While checking out a lead about Di, a posse led by Butte County Sheriff Ball and Colusa County Sheriff Beville came across a woodcutter's camp above Butte City. As posse members entered the shack, a man of Chinese heritage ran out the backdoor and was promptly gunned down. It wasn't Di.

On May 22, sewing machine salesman A. L. Schubert, captured Hong Di in a grain field near Gridley in Butte County. Di spent a couple of days in the jail in Oroville before being extradited to Colusa for trial.

A trial was set for July 10 in Colusa, thirty-seven miles south of St. John, with Judge Bridgeford presiding. Di could not find an attorney to represent him. On the day of his trial, he finally acquired an attorney, who filed a motion of continuance so he could prepare for the defense. Judge Bridgeford outrageously denied the motion, and as the trial proceeded, no evidence was presented in Di's defense.

Later that evening, the jury found Di guilty, but two jurors, H. K. Gay and Mathew Edge held out for a lesser sentence than the death penalty. On the basis of California law, the judge was forced to oblige, and he sentenced young Di to life in prison. The crowd in the courtroom went wild; many drew their pistols and shook them in the air before Judge Bridgeford was able to restore order.

The citizens of Colusa County were wild for blood. The Colusa County Guard was mustered to stand watch at the jail. There was talk of tarring and feathering jurists Gay and Edge, and Gay had the misfortune to ride the same train back to St. John as the Billiou family. During the short ride, he was punched in the eye and allegedly knocked off his feet by Maude Billiou.

Governor Bartlett sent the local militia to Colusa to stop the lynching of Hong Di, but when they arrived local merchants refused to sell them ammunition. *(California State Library Photograph Collection)*

As the night went on, groups of men huddled on street corners. William Weaver, whom Di had shot and wounded, stood watch in front of the jail, holding a noose in his hands while he boisterously led the call to lynch Di. Sledgehammers were the latest fashion accessory for the crowd of over a hundred angry men who had arrived on the train from St. John. The leading citizens of Colusa held a not-so-secret meeting in a prominent Colusa businessman's office. Sheriff Beville telegraphed Governor Bartlett to send the local militia to Colusa, but when they arrived, local merchants refused to sell them ammunition.

A jail guard casually told a *Sacramento Bee* reporter that he expected the jail to be overrun by the mob. The authorities knew that they couldn't expect the members of the Colusa Guard or the guards at the jail to fire upon their own family members, friends, and neighbors over a teenage murderer from halfway around the world. The best that Sheriff Beville could do was to hide the shackled boy in a crawlspace underneath the sheriff's desk. The sheriff then stood in front of his men and reportedly announced, "Gentlemen, in the name of the people of California, I ask that every man go down the stairs. I know the public feeling, and I am with it."

Led by a young bartender named Bud Welch, the mob chanted, "Hang him!" The lynch mob numbered over one hundred and fifty angry men. As they approached the jail, Sheriff Beville dismissed the Colusa Guard and turned the keys of the jail over to the rabble. The jail was searched and eventually the doomed Di was found under the trapdoor.

The crowd yelled and howled as Di was pushed out onto the streets of Colusa with scores of guns trained upon him. Di was pushed and shoved by the mob through Colusa's Chinatown, representing an unmistakable warning to the Chinese immigrants who made Colusa their home.

The mob stopped at a livery stable, where they intended to hang Di. They soon changed their minds and instead picked up the terrified teenager and carried him off over their heads, running to the Colusa and Lake Railroad yard. A rope was thrown over the rafters of the locomotive turntable and a noose was put around Di's neck. Weaver was called over to talk to Di, who was hysterically talking in Chinese.

"Why did you kill Mrs. Billiou?" Weaver allegedly asked.

"I was drunk," Di responded.

Di was yanked up by the neck at ten minutes to midnight, and he twisted in the wind for five minutes as the crowd cheered. He was let down and a physician was called. The doctor announced that Di's heart was still beating.

The crowd of two thousand spectators cheered, "Swing him up!"

Di was yanked back up into the rafters of the turntable, where he hung until he was dead. The crowd gave three rousing cheers to the leaders of the mob.

The mob now called for the jurors Gay and Edge, as they returned to town from the depot and no doubt headed for the saloons. The mob fired their guns into the air, calling the jurors, who had wisely removed themselves far away from Colusa. The mob marched back to the courthouse steps and gave three cheers for the Colusa Guards and three grunts to the jury.

Justice served, California style.

While Hong Di committed a heinous crime and obviously deserved his fate, the workings of the law were far less merciful to the terrified and intimidated Chinese community in general. Justice is traditionally reported to be blind, but in this case, the larger ramifications of law enforcement were certainly not color-blind.

Chapter 15

Twistin' in the Wind in Redding

Death Toll: 3

July 24, 1892, Redding—Shasta County

Although their father was a prosperous man, the Ruggles boys couldn't seem to steer themselves clear of Wells Fargo wagons. While it is true that "boys will be boys," these two young men failed to give up the antics of childhood, and, as a result, the citizens of Redding went to church on a summer Sunday morning without them.

John and Charles Ruggles were born in 1860 and 1871, respectively, to prosperous parents near Woodland in Yolo County. Their father Lyman had immigrated to California during the Gold Rush in 1850 and worked the mines until he realized that there was more money to be made as a farmer. The hordes of people tromping around California needed to eat, and the restaurants that popped up all over the state needed fresh produce and meat. In time, Lyman was elected to the Yolo County Board of Supervisors. Having an eye for opportunity, he started farming in Tulare County and eventually acquired over four hundred acres of prime farmland.

Young John was sickly, and so his father sent him to live in Stockton, closer to his doctor. John's physician, E. A. Stockton gave him a job as a stock tender on his ranch. John Ruggles had shown no inclination toward criminal behavior, but on October 31, 1878, he unexpectedly attempted to rob a couple who were out for a stroll. The man he tried to rob pulled out a revolver and fired five shots, hitting John in the back. Although seriously wounded, John surrendered to the police immediately; he quickly

In 1891, these gents were probably the best-dressed men in Yolo County. *(California State Library Photograph Collection)*

recovered and was tried and convicted for robbery and assault. He was sent to San Quentin prison for seven years.

Lyman Ruggles was distressed about his son's surprising crime and imprisonment. No sooner had the prison doors slammed behind John Ruggles than old man Ruggles started a campaign to get his son pardoned, which no doubt included large donations to the governor's campaign chest. Dr. Stockton wrote that he had been treating John for sex addiction and that John was nearly an imbecile when he committed the crime.

Governor George C. Perkins pardoned John Ruggles after he had served fourteen months in San Quentin. He was placed in the custody of his parents, and he seemed to go straight, working hard on his father's farm, eventually buying several parcels of property near the town of Dinuba. By 1887, he was married and had a daughter, but luck was something that was always just out of reach for John Ruggles. His wife took ill and died in 1889, devastating Ruggles. Unable to care for a young child, he left his daughter with relatives. With little to live for, he neglected his crops, spending his time hunting and living off the land in the Sierra Nevada mountains.

In 1892, John's little brother Charlie came to visit his brother in the mountains. Charlie had just come back from the goldfields in Shasta County where, instead of panning for gold, he had allegedly robbed sixteen stage-coaches in the area with a buddy, Arizona Pete.

After listening to Charlie's tales of his stagecoach robbing exploits, John couldn't resist hitting the outlaw trail with his little brother. He leased out his farm to a neighbor and rode north, stopping first in San Francisco for a little merrymaking.

On May 10, 1892, the Ruggles boys robbed the Weaverville stage, but the take was small. However, they decided to wait a few days before trying another robbery, while scoping out a new location where the road topped out over a hill, five miles north of Redding. It was a perfect place to stage a holdup, because not only would the coach be traveling slowly as it reached the top of the hill, but the horses would be tired.

The brothers stopped the stagecoach and demanded that the driver throw down the Wells Fargo boxes. As the second box hit the ground, simultaneous gunshots rang out and Charlie Ruggles was hit with buck-shot fired by a guard riding in the coach with the passengers. More shots rang out, and the air was filled with gunsmoke and the dust kicked up by the panicked horse team. A passenger named George Suhr was hit by buckshot, as was the driver, Johnny Boyce. The guard, Amos "Buck" Montgomery, was also seriously injured and bled profusely in-side the coach.

John Ruggles was shocked that his second holdup had gone so wrong. He ran up to the coach and fired his revolver into the already wounded Buck Montgomery's back. Immediately thereafter, Johnny Boyce regained control over his team, and he drove hell-bent for leather out of the area.

John ran to his brother Charlie, who was reeling from his wounds. He had been shot in the face and was covered in blood. Believing that Charlie was as good as dead, John grabbed the money, said goodbye to his little brother, and fled the scene.

Charlie was soon found by a posse and was taken for medical atten-tion. He had been struck by thirteen pieces of buckshot, with the most serious wounds knocking out some teeth and exiting his neck.

Charlie refused to tell the authorities who his partner was, but Wells Fargo detective John Thacker quickly figured it out and was soon on his way to see Lyman Ruggles, who was now managing a warehouse in Traver. Lyman caught the next train to Redding and visited his son in jail, where

Charlie admitted that his partner was his brother, John. An eleven hundred dollar reward was put on John's head.

John worked for a farmer for a few days and then ended up in his old hometown of Woodland, where the locals immediately recognized him. While he was eating a meal at the Opera Restaurant, Deputy Sheriff Wyckoff walked in, sat down at the table next to John, and leveled his pistol at the outlaw's head. Following a brief and inconsequential struggle, John was on his way to the Redding jail.

At the Redding jail, John was joyously surprised when he discovered that his little brother was not dead. They had a tearful reunion behind bars.

When they went on trial on July 28, the pair's strategy was to implicate the late Buck Montgomery as a collaborator in the robbery. This disgusted the people of Redding, as many of them had known Montgomery, and many had attended his funeral. There was talk of forming a lynching party and a scathing editorial printed in the *Republican Free Press* did nothing to help calm the situation.

In the early morning hours of Sunday, July 24, a group of masked men entered the jail and broke into the prisoners' cells. John tried to take all the blame for the crime to save Charlie, but the lynch mob showed no sympathy to the elder brother's final pleas. They hung the Ruggles brothers from a makeshift gallows near Etter's blacksmith shop. The purple faces of the brothers twisted slowly in the wind, greeting the townspeople of Redding on their way to church.

John and Charles Ruggles were incompetent stagecoach robbers who killed a popular Redding resident during a holdup. The brothers were taken out of the Redding jail and lynched early on a Sunday morning, July 24, 1892.
(California State Library Photograph Collection)

In nineteenth-century California, Wells Fargo wagons were a powerful temptation to men with limited judgment and little character. However, those wagons carried more than gold dust and greenbacks— they carried human passengers. And, when blood was spilled during a robbery attempt, California justice made sure "there was hell to pay."

Chapter 16

Rage Against the Railroad

Death Toll: 6; Wounded: Numerous

May 28, 1893, Tulare County

The California railroad companies had the force of the law on their side, but many farmers and landowners in the San Joaquin Valley resented the ruthless and sometimes heartless techniques of the railroads to protect and expand their interests and their vast wealth. As a result, swords would clang and heads would roll.

John Sontag was born in 1860 in Minnesota, with the given name of John Constant. His father died when he was four years old, and the boy took his stepfather's surname after his mother remarried. At age eighteen, he moved to California with his brother George and found work near Fresno as a brakeman on the Southern Pacific Railroad. In 1887, his ankle was crushed when it was caught between two cars. He was discharged from the company hospital in Sacramento before he was fully healed. As was the usual practice in those days, he was fired from the railroad without compensation because he requested lighter duty. As a result, Sontag held a grudge against the railroad for the rest of his life.

In the late nineteenth century, railroads became the largest corporate profit makers in America. Railroad magnates earned fabulous wealth, often by exploiting workers.

While recovering from his injuries, Sontag met a fellow named Chris Evans who shared Sontag's anger with the railroads. Chris Evans was born in Vermont in 1847, but his family moved to a farm in Canada when he was a toddler. When he was nearly fifty years old, he left for California with a younger brother to try his hand at prospecting. After that endeavor failed to pan out, he settled in the San Joaquin Valley, married, and started a family. He would eventually sire seven children. Evans' first homestead was taken away from him when it was discovered that the title was invalid; the man who sold him the land didn't really own it. This was a common problem in the nineteenth century. The lack of accurate state oversight concerning land deeds enabled fraud to go unchecked. Evans farmed and worked at a bank until he saved enough money to open a livery stable in Modesto, but a fire destroyed his building and killed his stock. Subsequently, he worked land owned by his in-laws near Visalia.

California farmers were treated poorly by the all-powerful railroads, which charged them extraordinarily high fares to transport their perishable goods. Animosity toward the railroads ran high among the Valley farmers, especially after the 1880 Mussel Slough Massacre, during which five settlers were set up and killed over disputed railroad land titles.

While in Visalia, Evans met John Sontag and his brother George, and although he didn't trust them, he decided to join them in a series of well-planned train robberies.

On February 22, 1889, they robbed a Southern Pacific train at Pixley. When the Wells Fargo agent refused to open the express car, they attached explosives to the door and blew it off. The conductor, a brakeman, and an off-duty deputy sheriff made a counterattack but were quickly routed after the robbers' shotgun blasts killed the brakeman and nearly blew the arm off the deputy. The gang made off with $5,000 dollars in gold.

The gang laid low with their cash; they tended the ranch and raised their families. However, almost a year later, on January 24, 1890, they robbed another Southern Pacific train near Goshen. The robbery was going off without a hitch when a hobo, thinking it was his stop, hopped off a boxcar and frightened the bandits. They opened fire on him before they could see that he was just a harmless tramp. Despite the temporary snarl in the train heist, the gang collected $20,000 from the robbery and went back to continue their day-to-day routines on Evans' ranch.

A year and a half later, on September 3, 1891, the gang boarded a Southern Pacific train in Modesto and stopped it near Ceres. They fired warning shots to keep the passengers at bay before blowing up the doors to the express car. Inside the express car, the Wells Fargo agent attempted to prevent their entry, firing a couple of rounds from the smoking entranceway. A second bomb was thrown into the car, but it was a dud. By this time, several railroad detectives and train crewmen had jumped off the train and open fired on the robbers, who beat a hasty and empty-handed retreat.

Evans and the Sontag brothers, being the intelligent and thorough bandits that they were, made a new plan. A month later, they traveled to the Midwest and knocked off some express cars there. Not a shot was fired during these robberies and the youngest of the gang, George, wanted to stay in the area and reap the easy money. Evans, however, wanted to go back to California and his family, and John was homesick too. The gang headed back to the Golden State.

Just before midnight on August 3, 1892, the gang stopped a Southern Pacific train near their home town of Visalia. After blowing off the express car's doors with dynamite and severely injuring the agent inside, they made off with $15,000 in cash, $2,000 of which was useless Peruvian coins. The clever bandits had strapped dynamite to the locomotive's piston rod, disabling it and delaying any report of the incident. However, the Peruvian coins would become important evidence that linked Evans and the Sontag brothers to the robberies.

The railroads were powerful, and they could compel local law enforcement to do their bidding. The authorities received literally thousands of leads and officers started the excruciating job of questioning hundreds of suspects.

Following tedious investigation, railroad detective William Smith and Deputy Sheriff Ed Witty traveled to Evans' ranch to question him. They ended up arguing with his eldest daughter Eva, who insisted that her father was not there. One of the Sontag boys put an end to the quarrel by blasting the men with his shotgun. The wounded officers ran away.

That night a posse was formed, and the posse members staked out the ranch. The bandits had fled, but the authorities didn't know that, and they were stunned when at dawn Evans and the Sontag brothers approached them from behind and opened fire. Deputy Sheriff Oscar Beaver was killed in the exchange, although George Sontag was captured. Evans and John Sontag escaped.

George starting singing like a canary about the robberies the gang had committed, stunning the authorities. They had established no clear ideas about the gang in the first place, and they hadn't yet connected the various robberies. George Sontag was tried at Fresno and sentenced to life at Folsom Prison.

With the information they received from George Sontag, the authorities swooped down on Evans' farm and discovered the Peruvian coins, along with bags of cash buried in the barnyard. Evans and John Sontag were indicted for murder and robbery in absentia, but such hatred for the railroads existed in the Fresno area that nobody came forward with information on the whereabouts of the pair.

One person did eventually inform on the pair, but the posse appeared to have been set up. Sontag and Evans were aware of the raid and ambushed the posse as it approached an old mining claim that Evans owned near Sampson's Flat, killing the leader of the posse, former Texas Ranger Coke Wilson, and deputy sheriff Andy McGinnis. The bandits wounded Deputy Ed Witty once again.

For ten months, the men hid from posses, living in the wilderness near what is now Sequoia National Park. They hunted and fished for food and took shelter in the many caves in the area. They had many admirers, and the locals were happy to feed and shelter them when necessary. Evans and Sontag even came home to Evans' ranch for the holidays, although the authorities were not aware of it at the time. When Detective Smith learned of the holiday visit, he posted around-the-clock guards at the ranch. That infuriated the bandits so much that in April 1893, they stopped a stagecoach believing that Smith and some of his men were aboard. When they realized that their antagonist was not among the passengers, they let the coach go without robbing it.

Evans mailed his wife a letter, in care of the *Fresno Expositor*, and the editors published it. Even though George had admitted the gang's crimes, the populace still admired the gang and continued to be tight-lipped about the whereabouts of Evans and John Sontag.

On May 26, the outlaws ambushed another posse, wounding one member. The posse retreated but soon regrouped, and on May 28 they again crept up to Evans and Sontag's hideout and laid an ambush for the outlaws. The fourteen-man posse opened fire on the robbers as they were returning from scavenging, shooting their horses out from under them. Evans was wounded in the leg. The men struggled to shelter behind a manure pile and used it for cover as they traded shots with the posse until nightfall.

Both Evans and Sontag were wounded and bleeding. Sontag had six bullet holes in him and didn't have the strength to escape. Evans used the cover of night to crawl six miles through the brush to a sympathetic neighbor's home. At dawn, the lawmen rushed Sontag, only to find him near death. They stopped and had their picture taken with him before they carted him to jail, where he died of tetanus and peritonitis on July 3.

Evans' bloody trail was easy to track and he was quickly apprehended. He recovered in the Fresno County jail, but he lost an arm and an eye.

To raise money for Evans' defense, his wife and daughter Eva joined the cast of a play based on the exploits of their loved ones, "The Collis Train Robbery," which was performed in San Francisco. They packed the house, much to the dismay of the local clergy.

Evans was tried and convicted in Fresno on December 13, 1893, and sentenced to life imprisonment, but once again his daughter Eva came to her father's aid. She persuaded Ed Morrell, the waiter who brought Evans his daily meals, to smuggle a gun to her father and take him to safety. As Morrell was entering the jail, he panicked and shot Chief of Police J. D. Morgan. Morrell's team of horses spooked and fled before Evans could make it to the street. However, the pair horsejacked another team and made off into the night.

Morrell and Evans robbed waiting passengers at the Fowler depot on January 11, 1894, and again traded shots with posses around their Camp Badger hideout. Evans' arch-nemesis Detective Smith planted a rumor that Evans' youngest daughter was dying of diphtheria. When the outlaws caught word of it, they naturally returned to the ranch. They were caught in the trap and gave up without a fight. Evans was sent to Folsom and Morrell was given life, but was paroled in 1908. Chris Evans was paroled in 1911 and died penniless in a county poorhouse in 1917.

> *Due to their ruthless business tactics, railroad companies were highly unpopular in nineteenth-century California. And, because they were so successful at depleting chunks of the wealth of the railroad companies, Chris Evans and the Sontag brothers became folk heroes in the San Joaquin Valley. However, their actions were serious, deadly, and criminal, and they could not elude California justice forever.*

Chapter 17

Unhappy Days at Happy Camp

Death Toll: 2

December 5 and 14, 1894, Happy Camp and Fort Jones—Siskiyou County

As was often the case, Native Americans accused of crimes, especially against Caucasians, seldom made it to the courtroom in early California.

Approximately seventy-two miles west of Yreka, on the winding Klamath River and surrounded by the Klamath National Forest area is the village of Happy Camp. It seems hard to believe, but Happy Camp was even more isolated in 1894 than it is now.

Seven employees of local land owner F. D. Fraser walked out of the backwoods on December 5, 1894, and into Happy Camp to buy clothes. The ditch diggers were no doubt happy to have the day off from their drudgery, and some of the men got stinking drunk.

The men stumbled back to their work camp near Grider Creek in two groups of three. A twenty-four-year-old Native American named Billy Dean walked closely behind the rearmost group. One of the workmen was so intoxicated that his coworkers, William Baremore and George Taylor, left him at the Chinese-operated opium den located below the town on the Klamath River. It is not known what the men did in Happy Camp besides purchasing some clothing and getting inebriated on alcohol or perhaps opium. Nobody knows what else went on between the men—if they gambled, quarreled, or fought. There is also no record of how Billy Dean was treated by the Caucasians he worked with. In the late nineteenth century, Native Americans were still looked upon by the European Americans as tamed savages.

Billy Dean grew up in a cabin near the Klamath River. The locals considered him an evil person who was not beyond committing burglary and arson. He was blamed for many crimes, but there was never enough evidence to charge him. Whether or not Billy Dean ever actually did anything illegal is unclear, but it is easy to believe that young Dean had been mistreated by Caucasians all of his life.

Fort Jones was a wilderness settlement in 1870. *(Siskiyou County Museum)*

Near the Grider Creek Bridge, Baremore and Taylor sat down to rest. "Indian Billy," as Billy Dean was known to his workmates, pulled out a revolver and shot Baremore in the right temple, splattering his brains upon the freshly fallen snow. Dean then fired two shots into the air before throwing the pistol into the river.

After walking back to Happy Camp, Dean turned himself in to the authorities. On December 8, a preliminary examination was held during which Dean claimed that the pistol fired accidentally. The men were so intoxicated on booze (and possibly opium) that it is quite probable that it was indeed an accident.

There was talk around Happy Camp of dealing out vigilante justice, so Constable Fred Dixon slipped Dean out of Happy Camp for his safety on December 11, with the intention of harboring the prisoner in the Yreka jail where his trial was to be held. Dixon and Dean arrived in the settlement of Fort Jones, where they felt safe, and took a hotel room for the night.

Constable Dixon and Dean shared a room with a man named Joseph Morrison. Morrison got into one bed, while Constable Dixon and Dean shared the other. If Joe Morrison intended on getting any sleep that night, he was in for a rude awakening.

At about two in the morning, a dozen masked men burst into the room and quickly disarmed Constable Dixon. They tied Dean's hands and carried him down the street to the Wheeler Building, which was under construction. The masked men had everything they needed for a lynching ready at the construction site. A rope, holding a block and tackle, dangled from the derrick, with a shorter, skillfully made noose suspended below it. Dean was summarily strung up.

Dean's body was left hanging until eleven o'clock in the morning of December 12, so that the citizens of Fort Jones would learn what happens to murderers in Siskiyou County.

The headlines of the December 14, 1894, *Scott Valley News* boasted, "He Is Now A Good Indian. Billy Dean Kills a White Man Without Cause and Is Summarily Hoisted to the Happy Hunting Ground." And thus, another shameful case of lynching entered the annals of California history.

For Billy Dean, "justice" came to be an "example," rather than a "right." Whether deserved or not, Billy's fate certainly was not determined by a jury of "his peers."

Chapter 18

Too Many Guests at the Jailhouse

Death Toll: 9

August 26, 1895, Yreka—Siskiyou County

When the county jail of Siskiyou County began to fill up with murderers awaiting trial in the late summer of 1895, the tax-paying citizens ran out of patience. The cost of maintaining the prisoners obviously outweighed the normal demands of the processing of justice.

Lawrence H. Johnson was a Scottish emigrant who worked hard at various jobs around Etna, a mining town west of Yreka. His work often took him away from home overnight, which left his wife alone. The fifty-nine-year-old Johnson had a feeling that his wife was unfaithful while he was away, so on the night of July 28, 1895, Johnson kissed his wife goodbye and then hid out near his home to see if his worst fears were true. They were.

Johnson saw a young man enter his home. After waiting a short time, Johnson entered his home and found his wife in bed with her young lover. Johnson pulled out his revolver and started firing at the young man, who jumped out of the window. The only thing that saved the young Romeo was that Johnson's gun misfired all three times he pulled the trigger.

Turning his anger onto his adulterous wife, Johnson pulled out his huge Bowie knife and stabbed her four times in the chest and stomach. Why she hadn't jumped out of the window to save herself is unknown.

Feeling remorse for the death of his wife, Johnson turned himself in to the Sheriff I. A. Moxley of Etna. Johnson's only regret was that his pistol had misfired. Sheriff Moxley took Johnson to Yreka for the murderer's safety, as the people of Etna were in a lynching mood and Johnson was just another murderer trying the patience of the community.

Garland Stemler was on summer break from his studies at a southern California college. The nineteen-year-old Arkansas native was looking for adventure during his time off, so he rode the rails, traveling throughout the state in the guise of a hobo. During his travels, he met up with forty-year-old Louis Moreno.

Moreno was no college boy slumming the rails for a summer adventure. He was a full-time criminal hobo, ready to break the law to suit his immediate needs. On August 19, the mismatched pair were short on money, so they entered the Sears Saloon in Bailey Hill, fifteen miles north of Yreka, with the intentions of robbing it.

Saloon owner George Sears and his elderly German bartender, Casper Meierhaus, had no intentions of letting the hooligans make off with the day's receipts. A fight transpired that surprised the younger men. In the ensuing fight, Sears was shot in the head and died before he hit the floor. Meierhaus was shot in the stomach, but lived long enough to give a full description of his assailants.

The hobos split up and ran in different directions. Moreno was quickly captured, as he was the only Mexican running around Bailey Hill with a bullet wound in his hand. Stemler was arrested in the Pokegama railyard. He had a recently fired pistol in his possession that matched the shell casings left at the saloon. Stemler also had the bad luck of having made acquaintance with Meierhaus in the past. Meierhaus identified Stemler by name.

Ohio-born William Null was one of the thousands who came to California to try his hand at finding gold. The forty-five-year old Null had shot his partner, Henry Hayten, in the back on April 21 over a dispute about their claim near Callahan. He pleaded insanity and was cooling out in the Siskiyou County jail, awaiting his trial for the murder, which was scheduled for August 25. Both Moreno and Stemler took accommodations in the Yreka jailhouse.

The citizens of Siskiyou County and Yreka were enraged that their community suddenly found four murderers in their county jail. Disgusted at the fact that their tax money was being used to feed and house the murderers while the wheels of justice turned slowly, they decided to take matters into their own hands.

The working men of the county started leaving their jobs early on August 25. Their employers wondered why everyone was suddenly feeling ill, and wives around the county looked in vain for their husbands who had left their evening farm chores undone. The men hid out in the forest near Yreka, staging themselves as had been set out in the timetable that was organized beforehand. A jug of rotgut whiskey was passed around to instill courage in the normally upright and sober family men.

The men detained anyone who happened upon them and didn't know the password, which was "mud." The detained men had the choice to either join the party or be held hostage under armed guard. By nine in the evening, two hundred and fifty men drifted into the outskirts of Yreka. One squad of men went to a blacksmith shop and acquired the necessary equipment for a lynching—rope and sledgehammers. Another squad went to the railroad yard and lugged off a rail.

Another squad went to the fire station and tied the bell ropes too high to be reached without a ladder, so nobody would be able to raise an alarm. Other squads swept the streets of Yreka to corral any unfortunates who happened to be about, and these men were either pressed into joining the lynch mob or taken prisoner.

The masked men woke Deputy Sheriff Radford at his courthouse office and demanded the keys to the jail. Deputy Radford told the mob that he would blow out the brains of anyone who came through the door. The mob knew that Radford meant what he said and left a squad of men to keep the deputy at bay while they searched for a new way into the jail.

The younger men among the mob climbed over the stone wall that enclosed the jail yard, waking the night guard, Deputy Henry Brautlacht. Brautlacht thought that some prisoners were escaping and stepped out of the jail, where he was promptly captured and disarmed by a squad of masked men. They took his keys and unlocked the cell block. Not having access to the keys for the individual cells, the mob used sledgehammers to break the locks on the murderers' cells.

Around eleven in the evening, some men pounded on City Marshal Erskine Parks' door, and told him there was a huge fight occuring on Miner Street. The marshal left his home in his nightshirt and ran down to Miner

Street, where some men informed him that the fight had moved over to Main Street. When Marshal Parks arrived at Main Street and found not a soul in sight, he realized that he had fallen hook, line, and sinker for a diversion. Out of breath, Parks ran for the fire bell to raise the alarm, only to find the ropes beyond his reach. He ran to the jail, firing his pistol into the air, only to find the jail overrun by the lynch mob. He was outnumbered and powerless to stop the lynching.

By one in the morning of August 26, 1895, the jail cell doors were smashed open and a mysterious, middle-aged man wearing a long duster and a white mask appeared. He calmly ordered the mob to start their business.

A local photographer recorded the gruesome lynching of William Null, Garland Stemler, Louis Moreno and Lawrence H. Johnson near the Yreka courthouse at one o'clock in the morning August 26, 1895. *(Siskiyou County Museum)*

The mob leader gestured for wife-killer Lawrence Johnson to go first, and the mob dragged the pleading man to the railroad rail that had been wedged between the limbs of two locust trees. A noose was put around his neck and he was yanked up into the air in mid-sentence.

Next, the captain of the mob went to Null's cell. Null tried to make a statement before he was executed. His statement was cut short by the rope.

Moreno walked silently to the makeshift gallows. He showed no signs of fear and made no sounds as he joined Null and Johnson on the rail.

There was some talk between the leaders of the mob as to whether or not young Garland Stemler should join the others. It was decided that he was just as bad as the others and, because of his advanced education, he should have known better. Stemler was so frightened he could hardly speak. He asked the mob to remove his boots because he promised his mother that he would die with his boots off. He also said, "Tell my brother to tell my mother that I am innocent."

Stemler joined Johnson, Moreno, and Null in the locust trees, hanging like some kind of sick Christmas tree ornaments. Witnesses said that the executions had all been botched, and the ropes stretched and the men twisted as they slowly strangled to death.

The mob left as quickly and quietly as they had appeared. Marshal Parks and Coroner Scofield soon cut the bodies down. Around the neck of Lawrence Johnson was a note that read:

> "Caution—let this be a warning and it is hoped that all cold-blooded murderers in this county will suffer likewise."
> Yours Resp'ly,
> Tax Paying Citizens.
> P.S. "Officers, ask no questions, be wise and keep mum."

No one was ever prosecuted for the lynching and not a single person was ever identified as a member of the lynch mob. Legend has it that the two locust trees in which the men were hanged died a little more than a year after the lynchings. They supposedly withered away as if they had been strangled.

It was a rare incident in California history—the lynching, at the same time, of several men charged with unrelated crimes. Assumed: the savings of tax dollars assuaged the consciences of those involved.

Chapter 19

The Bandit with Soft Hands and a Hard Heart

Death Toll: 2

October 14, 1897, Delta—Shasta County

Even at the turn of the century, events in California could reflect its violent, lawless frontier past. While law enforcement was becoming increasingly efficient, life could still be dangerous and deadly. And, sometimes a trial became superfluous.

William M. Harrall drudged through life in northern California communities, living hand-to-mouth, working as a logger, miner, cowboy, railroad section hand, and as a laborer in the region's many sawmills. The young father worked at any job that would enable him to feed his family. He had a good reputation as a hard worker, didn't drink or gamble, and kept to himself, but Harrall could never make enough money to start his own ranch or business.

Harrall was born in 1863 on a farm in Wayne County, New York. When he was seventeen years old, he left his family and headed west to make his fortune. While he was gone, his entire family except for his father, Thomas, died in an epidemic. Thomas traveled west, looking for his only living child. It took him five years to find William, who was working at a ranch near Chico. A short time later, William moved to the village of Delta in northern Shasta County.

Life was looking up for William Harrall. He met a girl, got married, and started a family. By all accounts, Harrall was an excellent father and a loving husband, but he continually had a hard time providing for his family. He often left town for a month or more at a time, telling his family that he had obtained mining work at Cinnebar. In reality, Harrall was robbing stagecoaches all over northern California.

Harrall would efficiently disguise himself, and he wore sacks over his boots so his footprints wouldn't leave tracks. He worked alone, was polite, and only wanted the Wells Fargo money box. The witnesses could tell the police virtually nothing about the robber except that he had "white, soft hands."

Wells Fargo detectives alerted their employees to check local banks and businesses for a twenty-dollar United States gold certificate, which they knew had been taken in one of the holdups. United States gold certificates were rare in northern California, and most banks and businesses would remember if one had been passed to them.

Eventually, a Wells Fargo shotgun messenger found the certificate at the Bank of Northern California in Redding. The messenger bought the certificate and sent it to John Thacker at the Wells Fargo headquarters in San Francisco. It was eventually traced to a grocery store, where the store manager remembered a man who bought supplies and had them shipped to another man who gave his name as F. W. Lloyd, from Delta.

Wells Fargo detective Charles Jennings went to Delta to investigate, and he soon uncovered F. W. Lloyd's true identity. When he was certain that Harrall lived there and matched the descriptions that he had of him, Jennings sent for John Thacker to help with the capture.

A hearse in front of the Butte County Courthouse in Oroville around 1890. *(California State Library Photograph Collection)*

On October 14, 1897, Thacker arrived in Delta. He teamed up with Jennings, Deputy Sheriff George Stewart, and Siskiyou County Undersheriff William Radford, and the four men approached William Harrall's home for what they thought would be an easy arrest.

Harrall lived in a cabin located just a few feet from his in-laws' bungalow. Jennings covered the back of the cottage, while Radford served the arrest warrant, with Stewart accompanying him as a backup. Curiously, just previous to the arrest attempt, Thacker had returned to the railroad station to wait for the men and their prisoner.

Radford knocked on the door and asked Mrs. Harrall if her husband was in. She told the men he was present but closed the door. Seconds later, the door flew open and Harrall stood in the doorway. Stewart, who was standing behind Radford, said, "This is Mr. Radford." Radford told Harrall that he wanted to see him and held out his hand.

Harrall grabbed Radford's hand, knocked him off balance, and pulled him inside the house. With his left hand, Harrall pulled out his pistol and shot Radford point-blank in the chest. Radford tried to draw his own weapon, but he was as good as dead. In the last efforts of life, Radford grabbed Harrall around the neck and dragged him down. Stewart stepped through the door, pulled his pistol, and hit Harrall several times over the head with it.

While this was happening, Harrall's two-year-old daughter screamed while clinging onto her father's pant leg. Mrs. Harrall screamed and held her husband's arm. Stewart, seeing that he had a clear shot, fired five times at Harrall, killing him, but not before Harrall shot Stewart in the leg.

Hearing the gunfire, Thacker ran back to the house, where he found the two dead men in a house full of gunsmoke. Radford's clothes were on fire from the point-blank gunshot. Thacker put out the fire and took the dead deputy home on the next train to Yreka.

Harrall was buried in the potter's field in Redding.

William Harrall led a double life. While he was evidently a hard worker, a good neighbor, and an admirable husband and father, his antisocial pursuit of ill-gotten gains resulted in a widow and a fatherless child.

Chapter 20

Pioneer Terrorists Meet the Crazed Lynch Mob

Death Toll: 5

May 31, 1901, Lookout—Modoc County

Seldom in California history were members of a lynch mob identified and charged with crimes. And, as was the case in the following account, their convictions were even more rare. Usually, public sentiment concerning criminal activities ran high, and sympathies usually ran with the lynch party—or, at least it ran against the men who were lynched.

Fort Crook was established on July 1, 1857, in Fall River Mills on the Pit River in Modoc County, for the protection of settlers against hostile Indians. It was scheduled to be abandoned on June 1, 1869, and Captain Wagner was assigned to the fort to oversee its decommission. The Indian hostilities in the area seemed to be under control, and Captain Wagner was in command of a skeleton crew of one cavalry company with which to man the fort.

Captain Wagner was something of a scallawag and he took up with the wife of a local Native American. When the fort was abandoned, Captain Wagner abandoned his Indian mistress, whose Christian name was Mary, to a soldier named Calvin Hall. Private Hall was mustering out of the army, and he intended to settle in Modoc County. For taking his lover off his hands, along with her two Native American children, Captain Wagner gave Hall a small portable sawmill.

Hall used the sawmill to make a living, but he eventually sold it and settled on some land near the present town of Lookout. The couple raised her two teenage Native American children, Frank and Jim, who took Calvin Hall's surname.

Mary grew tired of Hall and took up with another white man named Wilson. They had a child together named Martin, but she left Wilson to take up again with Hall, who was raising Frank and Jim.

Sometime during 1900, a Native American named Daniel Yantes came to Lookout and moved in with the Halls. Yantes later took Mary away from Hall, and the couple went to live together on a ranch. Yantes was a detestable man who always carried a big gun, but he was nevertheless kind to the boys. Together, the two disreputable stepfathers shared the duty of raising the boys. However, everyone involved seemed agreeable to the situation, and they all made up one big, eccentric, extended family. It happened to be a criminally minded family as well, especially the boys, Frank and Jim, who were well known (if not yet convicted) for having committed a slew of crimes around Lookout. Caucasians, Mexicans, Californios, and fellow tribesmen alike viewed the family as psychopathic thieves to be avoided at all costs.

Calvin Hall had a knack for getting his adopted sons out of jail on technicalities, which made Frank and Jim even more daring and obnoxious. Whenever Frank and Jim were acquitted of crimes, the cattle and horses of the accusers were mysteriously killed or mutilated. Sometimes, the brothers would slash harnesses, burn crops, or destroy wagons. Frank and Jim were suspected of vandalizing a local schoolhouse, but there wasn't enough evidence to prosecute them. In the meantime, the locals assumed that with all the comings and goings at the ranch, the Halls' place had become a safehouse for itinerant criminals and fugitives.

This wobbly old jail in Bidwell Bar, Butte County, was typical of early California jails. (California State Library Photograph Collection)

In May 1901, a burglary was committed in the usually tranquil community of Lookout. The Hall boys were quickly suspected, and when the Hall ranch was searched, several of the stolen items were found. Branded hides and meat that didn't belong to Hall or Yantes were also found on the premises, and Frank, Jim, and Calvin Hall, along with Daniel Yantes and Martin Wilson, were taken to Lookout and placed under guard in the bar of the town's hotel.

Like today, judges and prosecutors were overworked and their offices were understaffed. Trials were expensive and the prisons were overcrowded. The prosecutor dismissed the burglary charges and ordered the men charged with petty larceny. Yantes Wilson, and the Halls, who would soon be out on bail, made threats of vengeance against the townspeople who had advocated prosecution of the criminal family. Everyone believed that the threats were serious. Houses and barns would be burned and throats could be slashed. The people of Lookout had finally had enough of the terrorist family.

At 1:30 A.M. on May 31, 1901, a group of masked men rushed the guards watching over the clan at the bar. They marched Daniel Yantes, Martin Wilson, and Frank, Jim, and Calvin Hall off to the Pitt River Bridge and hung them over the railings.

The people of Modoc County were shocked and encouraged the authorities to prosecute the members of the lynch mob. Modoc County superior court judge Harrington wrote to the California attorney general, requesting that investigators and a special prosecutor examine the case.

The grand jury convened on June 10 and indictments were presented against R. E. Leventon, Isom Eades, and James Brown. The case against Brown was the strongest, and he was "brought to trial" on November 21, 1901. Assistant Attorney General Post and Deputy Attorney General George Sturtevant were sent from the attorney general's office in Sacramento to prosecute the case. Ex-judge G. F. Harris, E. V. Spencer, and John E. Raker defended Brown.

Assistant Attorney General Post felt that he needed a bodyguard while in the wilds of northern California and he hired noted gunfighter Danny Miller to protect him. Miller generally made himself unpleasant to the people of Lookout during his stay. He bullied the locals and brandished his pistols at the slightest provocation.

The authorities were nervous that there might be acts of violence committed by the locals, and there was talk about bringing California national guard troops in to make sure that the peace was kept, but the only violence committed during the trial was caused by the assistant attorney general's bodyguard, Danny Miller. At one point during the trial, Miller drew a revolver in the courtroom and attempted to shoot attorney John Raker.

Bounty hunters and reward seekers poured into Lookout, hoping they could uncover evidence or persuade someone to testify and thus collect the reward offered by the state and several newspapers. So many residents were approached by the headhunters and pressured to commit perjury that popular opinion tilted towards acquitting Leventon, Eades, and Brown.

During the first week of January, a man who called himself Detective Gibson approached a young couple named Slavin, who were stranded in Alturas and were working for their room and board. Gibson offered the husband a percentage of the reward, about $900, to testify for the state. The Slavins told Gibson that they knew nothing about the lynchings and that as "poor as he was, Mr. Slavin would not swear to a falsehood."

Gibson returned a few days later, hoping that the cash would dull the Slavins' ethics, and he again tried to get Slavin to testify, explaining to Slavin that "the men were guilty and that no one would ever be the wiser." Slavin told Gibson that if he asked him to testify again, he "would shoot him like a dog."

The crooked investigators interrogated John Hutton and Claude Morris, who were also suspected as having been members of the lynch mob. The teenaged Morris was taken into a room, plied with whisky, and threatened by the detectives. At two in the morning, a completely intoxicated and frightened Claude Morris signed an affidavit that indicted fifteen members of the community. The affidavit had already been prepared for him. All he had to do was sign the paper.

The next day, Morris protested that he had been hoodwinked into signing the affidavit. He was told that he would be charged with perjury if he went back on the confession that he had signed before a notary public. The young man was not allowed to talk to an attorney. He was kept under guard and away from his family and friends.

On January 4, 1902, Mary Lorenz, the half-breed daughter of old Mary Hall, swore to a warrant charging fifteen residents of Lookout with complicity in the lynching. They were all arrested, placed in jail, and on January 10, indictments were filed charging each one with five different murders.

The trial was a farce. Judge Harrington disallowed any evidence introduced by the defendants' attorneys and "raved like a madman" against them when they tried to object. On almost every day of the trial, Judge Harrington sent one or more of Brown's attorneys to jail for contempt. Paid-off or bullied witnesses were paraded onto the stand to testify for the state, and Judge Harrington refused to allow the defense to produce evidence to prove the witnesses were lying. Attorneys Harris, Raker, and Spencer would argue the point and thereby manage to get the evidence before the jury. And, Judge Harrington would then send one of them to jail. The trial went on for months and cost Modoc County $40,000—a huge sum in 1901.

When the verdict was finally reached, the men were acquitted. The citizens of Lookout knew that the lynched men had been disreputable and dangerous characters. Both the witnesses and the reward hunters, who feared being charged with perjury or a necktie party, left town in the middle of the night. Assistant Attorney General Post and his bodyguard Danny Miller left Lookout on the first stage after breakfast.

The prisoners were discharged one, two, and three at a time, and quietly returned to their homes. Life went back to normal for the first time in a long time in Modoc County.

> In this case, it appears obvious that there was little real "justice" in operation at any stage of the proceedings. The lynched men, while detested in their community, received no trial. Witnesses apparently committed perjury. The judge turned the proceedings into a farce, and all of the alleged lynch mob members were acquitted. Yantes, Wilson, and Frank, Jim, and Calvin Hall paid a huge price for their deeds— as did the reputation of California justice.

Chapter 21

Bad-Ass Jim McKinney
Meets a Bad-Ass Shotgun

Death Toll: 5

April 19, 1903, Bakersfield—Kern County

---

*Bad men have certainly existed in every time period in history.
Jim McKinney was a psychopath and a cold-blooded killer whose
antisocial tendencies could be ended only by prison bars or a bullet.*

If Jim McKinney were alive today, he would certainly still be behind
bars, serving life without parole from the time he was twenty years old.
McKinney was a psychotic punk from Farmersville, a small town ten miles
southeast of Visalia. When McKinney was a young man, he pistol-whipped
a schoolteacher who had paddled his younger brother. After he had beaten
the hapless teacher to the ground, he pulled out his Bowie knife and cut
off a piece of the unconscious man's ear. A deputy sheriff witnessed the
violent act and ran to stop it. The deputy was successful in arresting
McKinney, but was slashed on the arm while apprehending him.

Nowadays, McKinney would likely serve a twenty-year stretch in San
Quentin for such a crime, but McKinney was acquitted in this incident. In
the 1880s, it wasn't uncommon for a criminal to be acquitted of such
straight-out violence, even with a police officer as the witness. California
justice was much more arbitrary in the 1800s than it could ever be now, no
matter how much politicians and the media complain about the current
legal system.

After the incident, McKinney wisely left Farmersville and became a
drifter. There were rumors that he had ridden with the Wild Bunch, of

Butch Cassidy and the Sundance Kid fame. He was also thought to have killed a couple of men in Arizona. One thing is certain: Jim McKinney was never a law-abiding citizen.

McKinney had a hard time staying away from California. He came back often, and he invariably caused trouble while there. In Visalia, he shot a woman in the buttocks when she wasn't interested in his affections. In 1899, he shot Long Tom Sears because McKinney's girlfriend told him that Sears had mistreated her. McKinney approached Sears in a Bakersfield alley and tried to provoke him into a fight. Sears, who had been a friend of McKinney, didn't want to fight, and he threw his gun onto the ground. It didn't matter to McKinney whether Sears was unarmed or had been a friend. The ferocious killer shot him down in cold blood.

As a bullet passed through Long Tom's body, Deputy Sheriff John Crawford was relieving himself in a nearby outhouse. Hearing the gunshot, Deputy Crawford ran out of the privy with his pants hanging down and ran directly into McKinney. The psycho shot him twice in the butt. McKinney was arrested and tried, but astonishingly he was acquitted of Long Tom Sears's murder and of shooting Deputy Crawford.

McKinney next appeared in the police ledger in April 1902, when he got drunk in Porterville and started taking target practice in Zalaud's Saloon. He shot the slowly revolving ceiling fan and, after becoming bored, he started shooting the liquor bottles behind the bar. A town marshal ran into the saloon and cracked McKinney over the head with a club. Getting whacked in the head wasn't enough to put McKinney down, and the mar-

shal was shot through his mouth, cheek-to-cheek. As the lawman laid on the floor in agony, McKinney stalked out of the saloon, but he soon returned, this time armed with a shotgun. He then fired with both barrels at the first person he saw through his booze-clouded eyes. Unfortunately, it was Billy Lynn, one of McKinney's few remaining

Plenty of bad men passed through one-horse towns like Porterville in Tulare County during the early days of California. *(California State Library Photograph Collection)*

friends. McKinney got onto his horse and rode out of town, shooting two men along the way.

McKinney hid out with his friend Al Hulse, who should have known by this time what happens to people who befriended McKinney. They hid out in a Chinese joss house in Bakersfield. It is hard to imagine a couple of hulking Caucasians going unnoticed in a Chinese temple for a year, but McKinney and Hulse managed to do just that.

On April 19, 1903, the police learned that McKinney was hiding out at the L Street joss house. Along with a posse of policemen, City Marshal Jeff Packard and Deputy Sheriff Bill Tibbet raided the joss house. Packard and Tibbet went from room to room while the rest of the posse guarded the exits. When Packard and Tibbet kicked down the door of the room where McKinney and Hulse were hiding, they were greeted by hot lead and gunsmoke. Packard and Tibbet were seriously wounded.

Rifle in hand, McKinney sprinted for the exit, only to run directly into the shotgun barrel of Deputy Bert Tibbet, the brother of Deputy Bill Tibbet. McKinney fired off a couple of wild shots before Bert Tibbet cut him down with his shotgun. Another deputy finished him off with a shot as he hit the ground.

Packard and Tibbet died of their wounds before the day was over. Hulse was arrested for harboring a fugitive. Seeing that most of McKinney's friends ended up dead, Hulse got a good deal.

> *Unfortunately, the California justice system missed numerous opportunities to put an end to McKinney's outrages, and at least five men had to die before a bullet brought a sudden halt to his nefarious ways.*

Chapter 22

Prohibition Mobsters "Hang Around" in Santa Rosa

Death Toll: 6

December 5 and 10, 1920, Santa Rosa—Sonoma County

The Eighteenth Amendment, enacted in 1920, was intended to benefit the American public. However, to a great degree, it promoted the growth and outrages of a particularly vicious brand of criminals.

On January 16, 1920, the Eighteenth Amendment went into effect, making the manufacture, sale, and transport of alcohol illegal in the United States. With America's most popular vice outlawed almost overnight, organized crime stepped in quench the nation's thirst. Crime rates reached epic proportions during the thirteen years of Prohibition, and mobsters raked in millions in untaxed income. With alcohol no longer regulated by the government, money, resulting from illegal sales, poured in like wine, and mobsters murdered each other for control of valuable turf on which to hustle their hootch. Criminal outfits often hijacked trucks transporting illegal booze, frequently injuring or murdering the drivers. Mobsters wanted by the law frequently hid out in small cities to wait for things to cool off. In some towns, the local chief of police took a payoff to allow wanted criminals to hide out unmolested.

Santa Rosa lowlife Terry Fitts was very familiar with San Francisco's notorious "Howard Street Gang. One of the first things that the recently released con did when he was paroled from prison was to look up his Howard Street buddies. Fitts had no intentions of giving up his criminal ways.

Fitts and his criminal buddies, "Spanish" Charley Valento and George Boyd, were wanted by San Francisco police for the gang rape of a young woman in Valento's Howard Street hovel. Needing a place to lay low, Fitts thought that Santa Rosa would be the ideal place to hide out from the law.

Evidently, the gangsters weren't flush with cash, because on December 10, 1920, they stopped at Pete Guidotti's home in Santa Rosa, where the hoodlums tried to borrow money from Guidotti. Guidotti refused to give them any cash, but his wife gave the starving men some soup. Nobody in Guidotti's home on Seventh Street knew that there was a squad of police from Santa Rosa and San Francisco surrounding the house. Police officers had been searching all over the seedy parts of Santa Rosa for the men and now they had the criminals cornered.

Detective Lester Dohrman and Sergeant Miles Jackson of the San Francisco police department burst through the front door, along with Sonoma County sheriff Jim Petray, but George Boyd grabbed Fitts's gun from a table and fired all of its bullets at the charging policemen. Sergeant Jackson and Sheriff Petray died where they fell, but not before Jackson was able to put a bullet into Boyd. Detective Dohrman died a few hours later.

"Spanish" Charley Valento, Terry Fitts, and George Boyd swing in the cold, dark Santa Rosa night on December 10, 1920. *(California State Library Photograph Collection)*

The gangsters bolted for the back door, but they were stopped by the dragnet. The seriously wounded Boyd was taken to the Sonoma County jail, along with Valento and Fitts.

Hordes of angry people congregated nightly at the jail, calling for the hoodlums' heads. Finally on the fifth night, hindered by no effort on the part of the guards to stop them, the mob broke into the jail and grabbed the terrified prisoners. They were driven to Rural

Santa Rosa crime scene investigators inspect the location of the lynching of "Spanish" Charley Valento, Terry Fitts, and George Boyd in 1920. *(California State Library Photograph Collection)*

Cemetery on Franklin Avenue and strung up, in their long underwear, from a locust tree near a cannonball-ringed veterans' monument. An inquest produced a verdict of "death by persons unknown."

It was believed that a mob of over two hundred masked men carrying weapons had overwhelmed the guards and made off with the unlucky gangsters, although rumor had it that San Francisco policemen actually lynched the prisoners. Some thought the lynching was committed by collaboration between local police departments and the seedy proprietors of Santa Rosa's speakeasies and houses of prostitution. Killing policemen is bad for illegal businesses, and getting rid of some of their own might have helped those shady businessmen make amends with the Santa Rosa and Sonoma County police departments.

However, sixty-five years later, a man came forth claiming he'd been the youngest member of the lynch mob. He said that a former World War I pilot from nearby Healdsburg led the mob with military precision and that they had drilled for three days before the actual lynching. When the mob reached the jail, they were given the keys to the jail cells by oblig-ing guards. The mob, which numbered thirty men in all, was supposedly made up of friends of Sheriff Petray.

Who lynched Boyd, Fitts, and Valento? It is unlikely that there is anyone still alive who witnessed the incident, and nobody will ever know for sure if it involved members of the Sonoma County sheriff's depart-ment, the Santa Rosa police department, the San Francisco police depart-ment, angry citizens, paramilitary hicks from Healdsburg, or mobsters tak-ing care of their own.

So many sightseers stopped by the lynching tree, carving off pieces of bark for souvenirs, that the city of Santa Rosa cut the tree down, much to the happiness of the respectable citizens of Sonoma County.

Ironically, the enactment of a "law" fostered a surge of criminality. On this particular occasion, some citizens, possibly including police officers, went "outside of the law" to bring "justice" to a small group of cop killers.

Chapter 23

A Dosage of Lead Is Administered on J Street

Death Toll: 2

July 2, 1932, Sacramento—Sacramento County

At times, justice arrives via the route of self-defense. In the environs of a violent locale, violent responses are often required.

Druggist Frank J. Quirin's store was located in a tough neighborhood, just across the street from Sacramento's Western Pacific depot on J Street. Hundreds of penniless hobos and travelers of dubious character would climb off the railcars every day, just a few yards from Quirin's Drug Store.

The neighborhood was tough, but Quirin was tougher. For over twenty years, Quirin operated his drug store on the 1900 block of J Street. He had been robbed numerous times over the years, so Quirin stashed pistols in secret places throughout his store. In 1904, Quirin knocked an armed robber in the back of the head with a paperweight before chasing him into the darkness. In 1911, a robber snuck up behind Quirin and put a gun to the back of his head before he made off with the till. The no-nonsense Quirin chased the robber into the darkness.

Quirin had many friends who were policemen, which came in handy during a robbery attempt in 1912. Three robbers found themselves facing both Sacramento police captain Ed Brown and Quirin and their loaded guns. They wisely gave up.

Notorious California robber London Bob robbed Quirin's store in 1922. Quirin went for one of the eight pistols that he kept on shelves and in various drawers and blasted away at the robber, knocking London Bob's gun out of his hand, along with his trigger finger. Quirin then put London Bob down with a bullet into his chest. Quirin was so intent on shooting London Bob that he was oblivious to the four bullets that the outlaw had plugged into him. Another robbery attempt in 1925 ended when Quirin pulled out a gun and shot at the man, who wisely fled.

Quirin hated the lowlifes who tried to take his hard-earned money and he often acted out to his police officer friends what he would do if he were robbed again. On the evening of July 2, 1932, Quirin's strategy didn't work out as planned.

Harry B. Campbell was a guy who never really had a chance in life. Born poor, with little education, he had been in and out of prison since 1909. His latest stint in the penitentiary resulted from a Los Angeles robbery for which he served eleven years of a twenty-five-year sentence at Folsom Prison.

While at Folsom, Campbell was a model prisoner and eventually became a trustee in charge of Folsom's ice plant. On parole, he had written Folsom Warden Court Smith, telling him how he had gone straight and was working at the Sacramento Ice Company at Fourth and R streets and was saving all of his money. He wrote the warden that he was pinching his pennies so much that he had not even gone to a movie since he had been paroled. He seemed to be getting his life together, so it was a complete surprise when he walked into Quirin's Drug Store with a semi-automatic pistol just three months after he was released from Folsom.

Not surprisingly, Quirin was not about to let Campbell walk away with his day's receipts, and Quirin went for his gun. He got one round off before his semi-automatic pistol jammed, and Campbell shot Quirin dead. Mrs. Quirin, who was just as tough as her husband, pulled out her own semi-automatic and fired off three rounds at Campbell, hitting him in the stomach. Campbell would have had been killed right there and then, had Mrs. Quirin's gun not also jammed.

Campbell fled out the door and, realizing after a few steps that he was severely wounded and would not be able to get away, he sat down on the on the Western Pacific railroad tracks, put his gun to his temple, and fired a bullet into his brain.

Frank Quirin was a hard-boiled entrepreneur who found it necessary to provide his own protection and to guard his property and goods from some of the "customers" who visited his pharmacy. At certain times, he and his wife were forced to fill a prescription with an element the intruder had not ordered—lead.

Chapter 24

The Governor's Mob of "Good Citizens"

Death Toll: 3

November 26, 1933, San Jose—Santa Clara County

Kidnappings have always been considered particularly odious crimes, especially due to the fact that the victims are almost never found alive, even after ransoms have been paid. Various high-profile kidnappings plagued the nation during the 1930s, and the citizens of San Jose had absolutely no patience with which to await the slow turning of the wheels of justice when a heinous kidnapping occurred in their city.

John Holmes and Thomas Thurmond were middle-class young men who grew up in the San Jose area during the Great Depression. Times were hard for almost everyone, and Holmes and Thurmond were lucky to have jobs. But honest work and normal lives didn't appeal to the young men.

Holmes was an ambitious and gregarious young man. Handsome and muscular, he had played football at San Jose High and was also a crime buff. Like many American youth of his day, he followed the exploits of Depression-era criminals like John Dillinger, Pretty Boy Floyd, and the Barker/Karpis Gang in newspapers and pulp magazines. Holmes analyzed the errors that tripped up the criminals and dreamed up better ways to commit crimes. Even though he had no criminal experience, Holmes believed that he could succeed where the most notorious outlaws of his day had failed. Subsequent events, however, would prove him wrong.

Married and supporting a family by the age of twenty-four, Holmes pumped gas for a living in Half Moon Bay. Although he should have considered himself lucky to have a steady paycheck when so many people were out of work, he hated his job. About the only thing he liked about it was that he met plenty of lowlifes and criminals who traveled up and down the coast between Los Angeles and San Francisco. He dreamed of getting lots of fast money by committing a perfect crime. But Holmes appeared to be all talk and he had never even been arrested.

By 1932, Holmes had worked his way up the company ladder and had become a salesman for the fuel company. On his route, he met Thomas Thurmond, an attendant at a San Jose gas station. Thurmond was a high school dropout and the black sheep of a popular San Jose family. He worked menial jobs and hung out on the fringes of the city's underworld. Like Holmes, he had criminal ideas, but he had never attempted to carry them out and had never been arrested.

The two men hit it off and became friends over their mutual fascination with making a fast buck through illegal means, and they soon settled upon the scheme they thought would catapult them into the criminal big leagues. During the Depression, criminal-minded folks came to realize that snatching some big shot or some rich man's kid could pay off, as there had been a wave of successful kidnappings throughout the country. Rich people like William Hamm, Jr., of Hamm's beer fame, and oilman Charles Urschel were successfully ransomed. Holmes and Thurmond figured they could pull a kidnapping off, too. Besides, they had seen it done in the movies.

Using inside information about the comings and goings of their company's messengers, they abducted and robbed couriers on September 25 and October 23, 1933, making off with a little over fourteen hundred dollars. Full of themselves due to their inaugural success, Thurmond and Holmes decided to go for a ransom kidnapping, and they quickly identified their target: Brooke Hart, grandson of a successful department store owner.

Hart's department store was known throughout the San Jose region as a place that sold good quality merchandise at low prices. Brooke Hart was an athletic and intelligent young man and was considered one of the most eligible bachelors in San Jose. The blond-haired, blue-eyed Hart graduated from Santa Clara University and drove a brand-new green Studebaker roadster. His father Alex had just made him vice president of Hart's department store operations. Surely, the aspiring kidnappers thought, Brooke would earn them a tidy ransom.

On November 9, 1933, Holmes and Thurmond put their new criminal endeavor into gear when they waited for Hart to leave a parking garage. Thurmond carjacked Brooke Hart as he was leaving the garage, sticking a pistol into his ribs and forcing him to follow the Chevy that Holmes was driving. Abandoning Hart's roadster in the hills north of San Jose, the three men drove to the old San Mateo-Hayward Bridge at the southern end of the San Francisco Bay. They forced Hart out of the car in the middle of the nine-mile long bridge, and Holmes hit the victim twice on the head with a brick. Then, the hoodlums bound him with wire tied to cement blocks and dumped him into the bay.

The ice-cold water caused Hart to regain consciousness and he began to scream that he couldn't swim. Thurmond pulled out a pistol and fired several shots at the desperate man, who quickly sank below the surface. Thurmond and Holmes had crossed the line from being kidnappers to being murderers.

At the time of the murder, Alex Hart was wondering where his son was. The elder Hart had never learned to drive, and Brooke was only going to the parking garage to get his car so he could drive his father to a business meeting. An hour later, Thurmond was on the phone to Alex Hart, demanding that he pay $40,000 for Brooke's release. Alex called the police, who at first thought it was a college prank. But everything changed when Brooke failed to return home after several days.

On November 11 and 15, ransom letters arrived instructing Alex Hart to take the $40,000 in cash and drive alone in the Studebaker toward Los Angeles. If he agreed to this demand, he was to put a large number "2" on a large sign placed in a window of Hart's department store. Because Alex Hart didn't know how to drive, he added in large black letters, "I cannot drive," to the sign he posted in the window.

At 8 P.M. that evening, Thurmond called Alex Hart at his home. Thurmond demanded that the payoff had to happen that night. The FBI had tapped Hart's phone and agents would be able to trace the call if time permitted. The police had Hart stonewall Thurmond on the phone until they could trace the call.

Dozens of law enforcement officers, including Santa Clara County police chief William J. Emig, raced to the traced address, which turned out to be a pay phone near a garage on South Market Street in downtown San Jose. Thurmond was still on the phone arguing with Alex Hart when the police arrested him.

After sixteen hours of interrogation, Thurmond told the police how he and Holmes had kidnapped Brooke Hart and thrown him off the bridge. He also told them that Holmes was staying at the California Hotel in downtown San Jose. Holmes was arrested without incident and both kidnappers were locked up in the county jail.

Sheriff Emig was afraid that some people in San Jose who knew the Harts would attempt to lynch the pair. The kidnapping had infuriated most of the residents of the county. The Harts employed hundreds of citizens and were well liked and respected by the community. In fact, just about everyone in San Jose had met a Hart family member at one time or another. Sheriff Emig and FBI agents took Holmes to San Francisco to continue the interrogation. Holmes denied any part of the crime, but agents soon persuaded him to cooperate, since Thurmond had already confessed.

The public outcry for Thurmond's and Holmes' blood was tremendous. Tapping into the historical spirit of California lynchings, the local newspapers were not shy about what they wanted to be done with the killers. "Let Justice Be Swift!" said one San Francisco newspaper. "Seek Noose For Hart Killers!" said another. A San Jose newspaper blatantly advocated lynching the men.

Police dragged the bay at the base of the bridge and uncovered evidence that Brooke had apparently struggled in the water for quite a while. He had tried to climb onto the bridge structure, scratching bird droppings off the concrete pier. They also found bailing wire with strands of Brooke's blond hair and cement blocks in the water under the bridge.

On November 16, two men found Brooke's decayed body on the mudflats a mile south of the San Mateo Bridge. Crabs and eels had eaten his face, hands, and feet, as well as his abdomen.

After Holmes and Thurmond were incarcerated in San Jose, Sheriff Emig had the jail locked down and secured. Large trucks were parked in front of the entrances to serve as barricades, but the crowds didn't assemble as predicted and security was eventually relaxed. That all changed on November 26, when the college students in the community went berserk with rage over the murder and surrounded the jail. Ten thousand other citizens of San Jose soon joined in calling for the blood of Holmes and Thurmond.

A nervous Sheriff Emig called Governor James "Sunny Jim" Rolph and asked him to provide California national guard troops to help guard the jail; his request was flatly denied. Sheriff Emig used all available police officers to guard the doors and windows of the jail, but they were outnumbered. The officers looked out the windows at the angry mob and saw friends, neighbors, and relatives arming themselves with pipes and planks. Mob members cut the phone wires to the jail and attacked the jail in waves.

Offices fired tear gas at the crowd, an action that only incensed the mob. Bricks and debris showered the building, as the crowd chanted for Thurmond and Holmes. Sheriff Emig ordered his officers to lock up all of their weapons on the third floor. He had enough firepower to kill everyone trying to break into the jail, but he didn't want that kind of blood on his hands.

Around eleven that night, the mob used a steel pole as a battering ram to bash open the door. They poured into the jail, pushing past the unarmed officers, physically beating some of them. The mob found a frightened Holmes shaking in his cell. However, before he was beaten to a pulp, Holmes was able to knock several of his attackers to the ground. They stripped him of his clothes and dragged him outside. Holmes was no longer in a fighting mood. One of his eyeballs lay dangling upon his cheek.

The mob found Thomas Thurmond hanging like Spiderman from water pipes near the ceiling of his cell. He too was beaten senseless and dragged outside. As the murderers were carried to Saint James Park, the mob threw bricks at them and took turns kicking and punching them. Panic gave Thurmond renewed energy and he fought back repeatedly, but he was always beaten down.

A noose was put around Thurmond's neck, but he managed to slip out of it. A few feet away, Holmes, who had never regained consciousness after being beaten in his cell, was strung up ten feet in the air. Thurmond continued to fight the mob until both of his arms were broken. He was then hoisted up into the air, kicking frantically until he strangled to death.

The crowd cheered wildly as the bodies of the kidnappers swayed gently in the breeze. Bright headlights from automobiles and flaming torches

Admitted kidnapper and murderer Thomas Thurmond hangs from a tree limb in downtown San Jose on November 26, 1933. *(Associated Press)*

illuminated the scene as individuals cut away whatever clothing was left on the murderers to collect as souvenirs. Taking clothing and even human body parts as trophies was a common action in the aftermath of lynchings.

A squad of highway patrolmen on motorcycles arrived at the scene and proceeded to restore order and to cut the men down. As the victims were being carried out of the park on stretchers, the mob continued to spit and punch the dead men.

The day after the lynching, Governor James Rolph expressed his approval of the double murder at Saint James Park: "If anyone is arrested for this good job, I'll pardon them all. The aroused people of that fine city of San Jose were so enraged…it was only natural that peaceful and law abiding as they are, they should rise and mete out swift justice to these two murderers and kidnappers."

Governor Rolph added that he would like to release all the kidnappers and murderers in San Quentin and Folsom prisons and deliver them to the "patriotic San Jose citizens who know how to handle such a situation." Although he had been elected to uphold the law, the "hanging Governor" allowed vigilante justice to prevail, in part to secure the future spoils of office.

Not surprisingly, given the sordid history of lynching in the golden land of democracy and freedom, nobody was ever charged for the cold-blooded murders.

> *Both the local newspapers and the governor himself became advocates and supporters of mob justice, and the infused sensibilities of the citizens of San Jose ruled the moment and sealed the fates of Holmes and Thurmond.*

Chapter 25

The Last of the California Cowboys

Death Toll: 1

July 15, 1935, Santa Rosa—Sonoma County

By 1935, Santa Rosa, California, had transformed from a frontier community into a twentieth-century city, and its streets were traveled by automobiles rather than by horses and horse-drawn wagons. However, at least one citizen could not let loose of the previous century image of life he carried in his mind. Tragically, his illusion led to lethal, "Old-West-style" gunplay.

Al Chamberlain was the last of his kind: a real live cowboy who had seen the frontier dissolve before his eyes and come to find his skills and lifestyle mocked by the younger generations. Born in 1858 to a Santa Rosa cattle family, Chamberlain grew up on a horse, roaming the rangeland and hills.

For several decades, Chamberlain owned a horse corral on Sonoma Avenue, where Santa Rosa's city hall now stands. He supplemented his income by acting as a guide and packmaster for hunting expeditions. Even though he was a living relic of a bygone time, many of the citizens of Santa Rosa, including some of Santa Rosa's finest, teased the old-timer.

In 1930, Santa Rosa bureaucrats forced Chamberlain to close up his corral because of allegedly unsanitary conditions. It seems more likely that the authorities were interested in condemning his property so they could acquire his land for construction of the new city hall. Chief of Police Charlie O'Neal personally signed the final notice to vacate the property. He gave

Chamberlain three days to leave. Chamberlain was never the same man after the eviction.

Chamberlain attempted to learn how to drive, but he was a horseman first and foremost. The sight of Chamberlain pulling back on the steering wheel of his old Chevrolet touring car and calling out "Whoa" caused the people of Santa Rosa to roar with laughter at the old man. He would often stop his car by crashing into the curb or sidewalk. Chief O'Neal warned Chamberlain to get his vehicle under control or stay out of town. However, Chamberlain wasn't about to let some badge-wearing bully tell him what to do.

One day, Chamberlain ran his car onto the sidewalk and knocked down a woman. She was unhurt and laughed it off, but Chief O'Neal threw the old cowboy into jail and charged him with reckless driving. Chamberlain was fined one hundred dollars and sentenced to thirty days in jail. O'Neal added fuel to the flames by taunting Chamberlain during the trial and tormented him by asking the judge to raise Chamberlain's fine.

After Chamberlain served his time, he started dressing again like the cowboys of his youth. He wore a big cowboy hat, boots, spurs, and old-fashioned flannel shirts. He had business cards made up that read, "Alfred E. (Two-Gun) Chamberlain, Santa Rosa Outlaw and Jailbird." He handed the cards out to everyone he met. And, he still drove his old Chevy around town.

Financially ruined by the loss of his corral and his month in jail, Chamberlain sold most of his ranch to John McCabe. He lost the rest of his fortune to back taxes, some of which were paid by McCabe. Chamberlain completely lost his mind and plotted to assassinate McCabe, Sheriff Patteson, Chief O'Neal, and his insurance agent, Harold Jones. He was sure that he would be lynched and would die with his boots on, like the cowboy outlaw he had turned himself into.

On July 15, 1935, a hot Monday morning, Chamberlain loaded his pistols and drove to his former home. At the ranch, he waited in the barn for McCabe to begin his morning chores. He then shot McCabe eight times, leaving him for dead. Chamberlain got into his beat-up car and headed for Santa Rosa, reloading his old nickel-plated .44 and .45 revolvers as he drove.

Arriving in Santa Rosa, Chamberlain parked his car and walked to the city police station on Hinton Avenue. Chief O'Neal was the only person in the stationhouse. Chamberlain pumped three rounds into O'Neal and walked out to find Sheriff Patteson.

The sheriff was at the jail next to the police station. He had heard the shots and he saw Chamberlain walking down the street with a gun in each hand. Patteson, thinking quickly, started walking toward Chamberlain. Chamberlain asked the sheriff, "Are you Harry Patteson?"

"Hell, no, I'm not Patteson," said the sheriff. "What do you want with Patteson?"

The men walked down the street together for a few steps when Chamberlain realized that the man he was walking with was actually the sheriff. Chamberlain raised both guns at Patteson and fired one of his pistols. Patteson tackled the cowboy and two men, Joe Schurman and Burnette Dibble, helped him disarm and subdue the old man.

That night, Sheriff Patteson took Chamberlain to San Quentin Prison for his own safety. The recent lynchings in Santa Rosa made it too dangerous to house the old cowboy in the Santa Rosa jail.

John McCabe recovered from his eight gunshot wounds, but Chief O'Neal died of his wounds on July 17. Chamberlain was tried in September and sentenced to life in prison. He died in San Quentin—a very uncowboy-like ending.

Sadly, Al Chamberlain could not adapt to a changing world. While it appears the colorful old cowboy was goaded into his violent final actions, gunplay on the streets was no longer viewed as an acceptable way to resolve disputes.

Chapter 26

A Bad Day at the Pool Hall

Death Toll: 2

July 25 through August 3, 1935, Yreka—Siskiyou County

While law enforcement was rapidly improving in many areas of California by 1935, there were still isolated communities patrolled by a limited number of lawmen. Also, California had a plethora of drifters and petty criminals who were anxious to take advantage of the situation. Times were tough, and virtually no one had it easy. Thus, normally law-abiding citizens had little sympathy when a murderous drifter fell into their hands.

The Great Depression was a worrisome time in American history. The stock market crashed and a drought hit the Midwest, disrupting the economy and displacing millions. Formerly solid citizens, farmers, and business owners were reduced to being homeless wanderers.

Robert Miller Barr and Clyde L. Johnson were just two of millions of jobless men who rode the freight trains around America, looking for work, a handout, or a petty crime to commit. Twenty-five-year-old Robert Barr had already served five years at the state reformatory in Ione and had been in and out of jail for a great part of his entire short life.

Clyde Johnson was born in Alabama and was a few years older than Barr. In the summer of 1935, he went on a crime spree, committing robberies in Hollister and Roseville, California. Johnson met Barr in the Santa Rosa jail and there the two cons decided to hit the rails together to reap ill-gotten gains in the mountainous extreme north of California.

Money was scarce in rural northern California in 1935. The local economy was based on timber and mining, but since nobody was building during the Great Depression, the mills and mines went quiet. The country folk grew or hunted their own food and bartered with their neighbors for other household items. However, they were able to eat fairly regularly, so in many ways, they had it better than a lot of city dwellers. That Johnson and Barr thought they could make a tangible score in such a poverty-stricken location attests to their lack of intelligence.

On July 27, 1935, Johnson and Barr rolled into Dunsmuir in southern Siskiyou County on a freight train. Dunsmuir is located in the Sacramento River Canyon, with only two ways in or out, north and south. Dunsmuir was home to a busy railroad yard, where trains picked up an extra engine to help pull the cars over the Siskiyou Mountains. Using their little remaining cash, Johnson and Barr booked a room in hotel near the tracks. They slept until noon the next day and had a hearty breakfast at the hotel's restaurant.

A photo of Clyde Johnson, apparently behind bars. *(Siskiyou County Museum)*

At a hobo camp, Johnson and Barr had learned that there was a pool hall that would be easy to knock off, located in the town of Castella, about ten miles south of Dunsmuir in Shasta County. They both put on stiff-brimmed straw hats and hiked the ten miles down Highway 99. There wasn't much traffic on Highway 99 during the Great Depression, and it wasn't unusual to see a couple of men walking down the highway, as the countryside was full of drifters.

The men sat down in the woods near the highway to wait for darkness. It was in the early morning hours of July 29 that they walked into downtown Castella with criminal intentions on their minds. Johnson and

Barr strolled into Padula's Pool Hall almost as if they were invisible. Two men were playing pool and four men stood at the bar. Johnson pulled his .30 caliber Luger and Barr pulled his Colt .38.

The robbers ordered everyone to put their hands on the bar, and Barr lifted their wallets, tossing them aside after removing the cash. They took the cash out of the register and ordered everyone into the back room, locking the door before they left.

Outside, they found a 1929 Chevrolet with the keys in the ignition and a drunk passed out in the back seat. They woke him up, paraded him to the back room of the pool hall, and locked him in with the rest of the patrons.

Driving north, they turned off the highway near Dunsmuir and drove into town via a back road. They ditched the car and their hats on a side road in North Dunsmuir. They had donned the hats as a diversionary tactic, figuring any witnesses would pay attention to their headgear and not their faces. Barr and Johnson figured the police would be looking for two men wearing funny straw hats and driving north on Highway 99. They headed for the local hobo camp to wait for the next freight to leave the yards, where they would hop a car and arrive in Oregon by first light.

The roads in Siskiyou County, around the time that Clyde Johnson and Robert Barr committed their crimes, were very primitive. *(Siskiyou County Museum)*

At least, that was the plan. Little did they know that the plan would soon go horribly wrong.

California highway patrolman George C. "Molly" Malone answered the call from Padula's Pool Hall. Malone was the sole patrolman in the Dunsmuir area. Although a competent officer, Malone asked Dunsmuir chief of police Jack Daw to go with him to the scene of the crime.

Daw's position as Dunsmuir's chief of police was an honorary title. The married father of three was a World War I veteran and a well-liked and respected citizen. Daw picked up Malone at Dunsmuir's police station.

The lawmen questioned the victims and looked for clues. After examining the tire tracks that led from the pool hall's parking lot, they were able to establish that the robbers had headed north on Highway 99. Stopping at every crossroad to check for tire prints, they found where the robbers had turned off the highway just outside of Dunsmuir, but they lost the trail after that.

Daw and Malone stopped by the Dunsmuir police station to inform the night officer, Joe Roderick, to be on the lookout for a 1929 Chevrolet with two men wearing straw hats, and then they headed out of town to North Dunsmuir on Highway 99.

Two miles north of Dunsmuir, the officers spotted two men walking south on Highway 99. Although they were looking for two men racing up the highway, not a couple of guys strolling along the road, they thought that it would be worthwhile to stop the men and ask them a few questions. Although the lawmen did not know it, the two men were Barr and Johnson.

Daw made a slow U-turn, crossed the center line, and pulled up to the men. Malone had a bad feeling and reached down for the submachine gun that had recently become standard issue to state highway patrolmen. As he was getting ready to step out of the car, Malone heard Daw say, "Get your hand away from the belt, buddy!"

Johnson suddenly opened fired on the car with his Luger, mortally wounding Daw, who slumped over onto Malone. Daw's foot slipped off the clutch and the car started to roll forward. Johnson jumped onto the bumper and fired into the back window, emptying his clip.

Malone, who was unhurt, saw that the car was picking up speed and rolling toward a gas station. He shoved Daw off of himself, grabbed the steering wheel, and maneuvered the car out of harm's way. He then drove

The town of Dunsmuir, during the winter after Clyde Johnson killed the popular Dunsmuir chief of police Jack Daw. *(California State Library Photograph Collection)*

away to get away from the gunmen, and he didn't stop until he reached the police station in Dunsmuir.

When the shooting had started, Barr panicked, dropped his .38, and ran into the woods. Unfortunately for Johnson, Barr was carrying all of the holdup money. An alarm went out to every volunteer fireman and auxiliary police officer in Dunsmuir. Dozens of armed men spread out looking for the killers. Johnson was quickly captured while walking on a side road.

Johnson was taken to the Dunsmuir city jail where he admitted that he shot Daw and told police who his partner was. There was talk of lynching among the rowdier elements of Dunsmuir, so Johnson was transported to the county jail in Yreka. In the meantime, every police department in northern California sent officers to join the posse for what would be a fruitless search for Johnson's accomplice.

Chief Daw was buried on a Friday, four days after he was murdered. An overflow crowd attended his funeral at the Dunsmuir Masonic Temple. The funeral procession then proceeded to a Methodist service, with an American Legion honor guard standing by. The distraught crowd of mourners mumbled in small groups. Between Daw's Mason and American Legion pals, there was talk of stringing Johnson up.

The members of the hardscrabble community were fed up with the rabble of wandering men, most of them decent people, but down on their luck and often desperate. The cold-blooded killing of an outstanding member of their community shocked them, and the failure of the search for Johnson's accomplice sat in their stomachs like a lemon. During the evening of August 2, a group of about thirty-five masked men piled into a handful of cars and headed for Yreka.

At about one-thirty on the morning of August 3, the men from Dunsmuir quietly walked up to the Yreka jail and knocked lightly on the door. When Deputy Martin Lange, the only guard on duty, opened the door a few inches, the men crashed into the entrance, trapping Lange behind the door. Lange, who was barefoot, was taken by two men to a car and driven away. The car sped through the towns of Montague and Grenada, some sixteen miles from Yreka, before Deputy Lange was dumped out on a lonely country road.

Back at the Yreka jail, the remaining masked men grabbed a large key ring and tried to open the jail door, but none of the keys would fit. They ransacked the jail office, breaking drawers and cabinets until they found another ring of keys. This time the keys fit the locks to the cell block.

The jail was full of inmates and none of them wanted to be mistaken for Johnson. The terrified inmates pointed the way to Johnson's cell. Johnson put up a fruitless struggle before his hands were tied behind his back, and he was led outside to a waiting automobile. A caravan of cars drove to a location approximately three miles south of Yreka, near an open-air dance club known as Moonlit Oaks.

A few hundred yards from the intersection of Fort Jackson Road and Highway 99, the masked men took off Johnson's shirt, tied his feet together, and put a noose around his neck. They jerked him four feet off the ground from the limb of a lone pine tree and tied the rope around a fence post. Johnson danced in the air until he strangled to death. Then, the men got into their cars and headed back to Dunsmuir.

Earlier in the evening, Deputy Sheriff Ed Mathews was serving as acting sheriff, as Siskiyou County sheriff Chandler was recovering from an illness and was bedridden. Mathews had been awake for nearly seventy-two hours, as had most of the police officers in Siskiyou County. As he sat down for a meal in a Dunsmuir restaurant, another deputy came running in to inform him that there was a lynching party heading for Yreka. The officers jumped into a patrol car and sped north on Highway 99 with their sirens blaring and lights flashing. It was two-forty in the morning, and they had an increasingly sick feeling that they would be too late to stop the lynching. Their fears were confirmed when just outside of Weed, the lawmen met a string of headlights heading south. Some of the car drivers honked their horns as they passed the deputies.

By the time the police found Johnson twisting in the wind, a crowd had assembled around his dangling body. The community had lost a beloved police officer, law-abiding citizens had committed a lynching, and Clyde Johnson was dead following a thirty-five dollar robbery from which he hadn't received a cent.

As for Robert Miller Barr, he was arrested on burglary charges in Los Angeles a year later. When the LAPD discovered he was wanted for murder in Siskiyou County, officers gladly gave him a ride up north to face charges.

Barr confessed to the police that when Johnson started shooting, he ran into the brush in the Sacramento River canyon. He had managed to flag down a car and got a ride out of California. He had traveled through Oregon to Portland, Klamath Falls, and a few points in between, sleeping in the woods for nine days.

Barr had then hitchhiked to Lake Tahoe where he found work as an extra in the movie *Rose Marie*, staring Nelson Eddy, Jeanette MacDonald, and James Stewart. Barr appeared in several scenes and his real name appeared in the credits. At the same time the film was being shown all over the country, Barr's face was appearing on wanted posters in every post office in America. Barr pled guilty and was sentenced to "life" at Folsom prison.

Clyde Johnson was not so lucky.

Many men were drifters during the 1930s, but Clyde Johnson and Robert Barr were "bums" in every sense of the word. Following a small-time robbery at a rural community pool hall, Johnson pulled the trigger and took the life of a small-town auxiliary law officer, and, as a result, he suffered the wrath of the poor, but far less heinous, citizenry.

Chapter 27

The (Not So) Brite Brothers

Death Toll: 3

August 29, 1936, Horse Creek—Siskiyou County

The Brite brothers often demonstrated consideration and kindness during their trips "into" town, but they were different men on their way home. Alcohol was the fuse and high-powered gun shells were the product of their final journey toward their mountain home.

In 1936, Siskiyou County was still suffering the effects of the Great Depression. The roads were virtually void of vehicles, as people drove only when absolutely necessary, but the steadfast, farming residents got by better than many people in the United States. Vegetables were grown, eggs were laid, and livestock was taken to slaughter. Neighbors bartered with each other for goods and services.

The great migration of Americans from the Dust Bowl states to California was in full bloom. Poor-as-dirt citizens of Oklahoma, Texas, and other states from Middle America streamed into California to start a new life. Most of these people were farmers whose own land had been rendered unusable as a result of years of drought and windstorms, so they naturally congregated around the large orchards and fields of the West Coast.

The Brite family was the quintessential Dust Bowl family. Archie J. Brite and his wife Martha "Ma," along with their sons, thirty-five-year-old John and thirty-one-year-old Coke, moved into an isolated mountain cabin, a mile and a half up a steep mountain trail, nine miles from Horse Creek, a village tucked into the rugged Siskiyou Mountains, about thirty miles northwest of Yreka, on the Klamath River. The only road leading to the Brite home was rutted Horse Creek Road, which predictably followed Horse Creek. The Brites would park their weathered and roofless Ford Model T at the trailhead and hike up a steep trail to their rented cabin, where they grew vegetables and did a little mining.

A typical miner's cabin near Horse Creek around 1900. *(Siskiyou County Museum)*

John and Coke were convicted felons who had served time in Arizona and Oregon jails before landing in Horse Creek. However, from all accounts, the brothers were polite and hardworking men. On their way to town, they often stopped at the handful of homes along Horse Creek Road to see if there was anything they could pick up for their neighbors while they were in Horse Creek. Because of the tough hike to and from the cabin, the sixty-five-year-old Archie and the sixty-four-year-old Ma rarely went to town with their boys.

The Brite brothers were always courteous when they went to town, but the thing that eventually got them into trouble was that they always bought a jug of wine to drink on the bumpy ride back home. When under the influence of alcohol, Coke and John had hair-trigger tempers, and they would become extremely violent at the slightest insult. Neighbor Charley Baker was a man who found out just how violent the Brite brothers could become.

In June 1936, after one of Coke's excursions to Horse Creek, he stopped off at the Baker place to drop off two loaves of bread that Mrs.

Baker had asked him to pick up for her when Coke had stopped by her place on the way to town. Coke's friend Maplesden, a local fellow from a pioneer family, was driving the Model T. Mrs. Baker could tell that Coke was drunk and told him that he should be ashamed of himself.

"No, goddamn you, Mrs. Baker," Coke said within earshot of Charley. "I ain't ashamed of what I done."

Charley Baker approached Coke and told him never to speak to his wife that way again and to get off his property. Coke responded by chasing Charley, cursing him with every step. Charley grabbed a heavy stick that was used as a rosebush stake and whacked Coke across the arm. Maplesden ran over to Charley and threw both arms around him, begging him not to hit Coke again.

"I'll get him out of here," Maplesden told Charlie. "I'll take him out."

Maplesden then ran to Coke, who was charging toward Charlie. The men ran around the house, with Maplesden grasping at the enraged Coke. Maplesden finally calmed Coke down and got him into the car. As they were driving away, Coke shook his fist at the Bakers and shouted, "I'll getcha!"

The next day, Charley drove to Horse Creek to seek advice from a friend. The friend told Charley that it was probably just the alcohol talking and that Coke would probably come over and apologize after he sobered up. The local justice of the peace, Judge Rainey, told him the same thing.

The Bakers had lived most of their lives in Long Beach, California, and had only moved to northern California a few years earlier. Charley, a retired carpenter, had few friends up in the mountains. He was a God-fearing, intelligent man, but he had a hearing impairment that sometimes made him quite cantankerous. Charlie and his wife were teetotalers, didn't socialize much, and were quite happy tending their garden. However, they were basically a city-oriented couple, and they didn't have much in common with the people who populated the Siskiyou Mountains.

In rural areas of the Siskiyou Mountains, deer hunting season was traditionally one of the biggest events of the year. Farmers worked to get ahead of their chores so they could have time to hunt. Hunting stories, mixed with good-natured kidding, dominated conversation in barbershops and restaurants. Deer hunting was as much a family "happening" as it was a sport, and it was always good to have some free meat on the table.

Vallejo resident Fred Seaborn was Charley Baker's friend and hunting buddy. For some years, the two had hunted together on the first week of the season. Seaborn, who was a retired naval officer and Vallejo's harbor chief, arrived at the Baker place on August 29, 1936, one week before hunting season was to start. He wanted to help Charley catch up with his chores and do some pre-season scouting.

After supper, the two men walked down to the trailhead to look for one of Baker's horses that had wandered off. They quickly picked up its trail on the Government Path and followed it down to a neighbor's pasture. It was a pleasant evening and the two friends enjoyed the stroll. It was getting dark out when they came upon Horse Creek, where Seaborn stopped to get a drink of water. In a few seconds, the lives of dozens of people would change with one ignorant act of aggression, fueled by alcohol.

Whatever precipitated the incident that occurred as the two men stooped to drink some fresh mountain water has been disputed since August 29, 1936. As Seaborn knelt to drink, he asked Baker who owned the old Model T parked at the trailhead.

Baker supposedly replied, "It belongs to the Brite boys who live up on the hill." Little did the men know that the Brite brothers were sleeping nearby, too drunk to have made the walk up the path to their home. And, interestingly, it was supposedly the only time that the Brite boys ever slept at the trailhead.

The Brite brothers, in their drunken stupor, had heard Baker's reply as, "It belongs to those two sons of bitches, the Brite boys, who live up on the hill."

Coke Brite answered, "You're goddamned right it does. What are you sons of bitches doing in our camp?"

An empty wine jug went whizzing past Seaborn's head. Captain Seaborn apologized in a loud voice into the darkness where the Brite brothers had been sleeping. Suddenly, Coke and John came charging out of the darkness and started a fight worthy of a Hollywood movie. Baker was beaten almost unconscious with a branch by John, while Seaborn held his own with Coke. Seaborn was a large man and a former sailor, who had seen his share of fights. Eventually, Seaborn and Baker got away from the crazed hillbillies and stumbled down the trail toward the Baker home.

Bloody and bruised, the two friends drove down the mountain road to Horse Creek to inform the authorities about the assault. Judge Rainey issued an arrest warrant for the brothers and called the sheriff in Yreka.

Meanwhile, the Brite brothers crawled back into their bedrolls and dozed off. Not long after they fell asleep, a hoot owl woke them up. John sat up and fired a shot from his .32 semi-automatic pistol in the general direction of the owl. That seemed to shut the bird up.

Deputy Martin Lange, Baker, Seaborn, and a former constable, Joe Clark, drove out to the end of Horse Creek Road with the intention of arresting the Brite brothers. Using flashlights, the men approached the sleeping hillbillies. Joe Clark walked up behind the Brite brothers' sleeping area and pulled the blankets off the men, which angered them to psychotic proportions.

Despite their screams and antics, Clark was able to smack John over the head with his blackjack a couple of times, which quieted the man. Coke arose, and Clark clubbed him in the head, too. As the men were being handcuffed, Coke made a lunge for the blackjack and Deputy Lange got him into a bear hug.

Baker and Seaborn were standing about eight feet from the fracas when the scrappy Deputy Lange and Coke landed in front of them. Seaborn hit Coke over the head a few times with his flashlight, pulled him away from Lange, and threw him to the ground. Coke landed on his bedroll and grabbed his .30–30 carbine and started firing. Baker was the only person, other than the drunken Brite Brothers, to make it out of the camp alive.

Baker ran to the home of his neighbor B. F. Decker, who lived only a few hundred yards from the trailhead. Decker immediately went to the camp and tried to talked some sense into the Brite brothers. He assured the men that he bid them no harm and only wanted to see what had happened. Decker found Deputy Lange on his back in the center of the road. There were two bullet holes between his eyes and one under his nose. Most of his upper jaw had been blown off. Lange had also been shot in the thigh, and he was barely alive when Decker found him.

Joe Clark was lying on the ground with his coat over his head. He had a bullet in this back and a carbine, now broken, was lying nearby. Coke had beaten Clark with the gun after he shot him.

Seaborn was lying on his back with his face smashed in. He had been shot under his left arm. Seaborn, like Lange, was barely alive. It was now B. F. Decker's turn to alert the authorities.

The Brite brothers ran for their parents' cabin and told them what had happened. Knowing northern California's reputation for lynching cop killers, Coke and John headed for the hills.

Decker fetched his neighbor and mining partner Bob Lanning and they headed to Horse Creek to find the justice of the peace. Deputy Sheriff Ed Mathews answered the call. Mathews had been the acting sheriff when Clyde Johnson was lynched in 1935. He had tried valiantly to intercept the lynch mob, but was too late. The last thing that Deputy Mathews wanted was another lynching during his watch.

Deputy Mathews called Sheriff Chandler at his home and told him of the situation. In short time, Sheriff Chandler, Mathews, Doctor Schlappi, Deputy L. L. Fortna, and Yreka city police officers Gilbert Rhodes and Frank Fullerton were screaming upward through the mountains toward Horse Creek in Mathews' car. In the meantime, Judge Rainey, Decker, Lanning, and Joe La Plant headed up Horse Creek Road to see if anyone could be saved.

At the Brite campsite, Sheriff Chandler made a surprisingly scientific investigation of the crime scene, preserving and cataloging the evidence. Ma and Pa Brite were questioned and their cabin was searched. They told the sheriff that the boys had fled into the mountains because they were frightened that they would be lynched. Nine separate posses were organized, and the Brite cabin was kept under constant surveillance.

Deer season was fast approaching, and the mountains and ravines would soon be full of hunters, who would also be on the lookout for the murderous brothers. With a handsome reward offered for the capture of the Brite brothers, some of the hunters were more interested in hunting the brothers than they were in their usual quarry. Several times, hunters collared unsuspecting prospectors, hoping that they might be the Brite brothers. In one case, a man was almost lynched after his captors took him to a tavern instead of to the authorities.

The Siskiyou County Courthouse in Yreka. Siskiyou County District Attorney James G. Davis burned the midnight oil in his office here during the Brite brothers' trial in 1936. *(Siskiyou County Museum)*

Such was the fever pitch to revenge the deaths of three men that Frank Merriam, governor of the state of California issued the following statement:

"There must be no more lynchings in California: I will take whatever action is necessary to enforce the law."

Siskiyou County district attorney James G. Davis had his hands full. Elected to the position only two years earlier, he had bested the incumbent by only 344 votes. He had kept silent the fact that he was half Native American during a time when Native Americans were still looked upon as subhuman in the rural areas of northern California. It was extremely rare for a Native American to even have a high school education, let alone college and law degrees. However, some people in the area didn't like the way Davis was handling the investigation into the murder and the manhunt. In fine California fashion, there was grumbling about a recall.

Meanwhile, trackers found fresh tracks that had been left by the brothers, and there was suspicion that the boys were provided with food and supplies by Ma and Pa Brite, even though their cabin was under twenty-four-hour watch. There was concern that the Brite brothers would come back and kill Baker, who still lived at his cabin, located less than a mile from the murder site.

As the pursuit continued, Sheriff Chandler, District Attorney Davis, and some neighbors were cozying up to Ma Brite, hoping that some sort of agreement could be made so that the Brite brothers could surrender and be protected from being pulled out of the Siskiyou County jail in the middle of the night and hung from a telephone pole by a crowd of masked men.

On September 17, District Attorney Davis scooted out of his office in a hurry. Nobody knew where he was going and why he was being so tight-lipped. Davis didn't show up for work the next day and the people following the case realized that something was up.

On September 19, Sheriff Chandler received a telephone call from the warden of Folsom Prison, located just east

A view of the Klamath River Highway (State Highway 96) at the time when murderers Coke and John Brite were smuggled out of Siskiyou County by District Attorney Davis and Dr. Harris. The Brite brothers were secretly taken to Folsom Prison to protect them from angry Siskiyou County residents. *(Siskiyou County Museum)*

of Sacramento. The district attorney and Dr. Earl Harris had arrived at Folsom Prison with the recently captured Coke and John Brite. They were to be imprisoned in the infamous penitentiary to await their trial. Having been on the lam for nineteen days, the Brite brothers had willingly given themselves up. They had met secretly with Davis and Dr. Harris, a dentist, at noon near the Brite cabin. The group had driven in a roundabout way to Sacramento, taking Highway One along the coast in order to avoid anyone who might recognize them. The trip had taken nearly an entire day.

A trial was held and the Brite brothers claimed many things, including that they couldn't remember the fight or the murders because they were too drunk. They also blamed Baker for inciting the fight by calling them "sons of bitches." The brothers were found guilty of three counts of first-degree murder.

On December 22, 1936, the men were sentenced to death; however, after years of appeals, the sentence was reduced because there were questions about Deputy Clark's sobriety at the time of the attempted arrest of the brothers and the credibility of the witnesses. Oddly, District Attorney Davis led the appeal. The brothers' sentence was reduced to life in prison.

A main street in the city of Yreka during the 1930s. *(California State Library Photograph Collection)*

The people of Siskiyou County were very resentful about the sentence and the actions of the district attorney. Davis lost his effort for reelection in 1938, mainly due to his defense of the killers.

The Brite brothers were paroled on September 17, 1951, but they both violated their parole orders and were returned to Folsom Prison. Coke Brite was paroled in 1972. He died on April 19, 1973. John Brite was reported to have been murdered in prison sometime between 1964 and 1973.

Some historians believe that Coke and John Brite were innocent and that Charley Baker, Fred Seaborn, Deputy Martin Lange, and Constable Clark had set up the brothers in order to gain access to the Brites' cabin for unknown purposes. This seems highly unlikely because Baker and his wife had only lived in the area for a few years and by all accounts were loners with few friends. Seaborn had a respectable job as the harbor chief of the city of Vallejo and was in Siskiyou County only to visit Baker and to go hunting. Since Baker already had a nice home, located less than a mile from the Brites' cabin, what would the men possibly want with access to an old ramshackle miner's cabin? And why would Constable Clark and Deputy Lange want to risk their careers and reputations by helping near-strangers, Baker and Seaborn, gain access to the cabin? The facts of the violent attack and the brothers' criminal records, along with their inability to hold their alcohol, also contradict that theory.

There is no doubt that the Brite brothers could have been lynched and that District Attorney Davis went beyond the call of duty in protecting them, but when the facts are all laid out it is obvious that the Brite brothers weren't very bright after all. In reality, they were ignorant, drunken psychopaths who would feloniously assault neighbors at the slightest insult, and they murdered three men at the end of Horse Creek Road in 1936.

The advice "Don't take your guns to town, boys" might have served the Brite boys well. In this case, California justice prevailed, and while the lives of the perpetrators of this violent episode were not summarily ended, their days in Folsom Prison could not have been so entertaining as their trips into town.

Chapter 28

What Goes Around, Comes Around: A Whacker Is Whacked

Death Toll: At least 8

June 20, 1947, Beverly Hills—Los Angeles County

If mobster Bugsy Siegel did not actually bring organized crime to California, he certainly refined its operations from his base in Los Angeles. Siegel was an incredibly violent and rapacious fellow, and, in addition to his other outrages, he did his best to corrupt the justice system. While the California justice system was unable to bring him down, Siegel finally transgressed the "law" of the Mob, and he paid the price.

Benjamin "Bugsy" Siegel grew up a poor Jewish boy in the slums of Brooklyn. Everywhere he looked there was disease, poverty, and crime. The tough streets honed his body into a catlike creature, alert and responsive. Before he was a teenager, young Ben ran extortion rackets in his neighborhood, demanding protection payments from street cart vendors. If the merchant didn't pay up, his cart would mysteriously, or not so mysteriously, catch on fire.

Crime obviously paid for Siegel, a handsome man who wore only the best and latest fashions. Siegel rose up the criminal underworld's ladder. He teamed up with the soon-to-be infamous mobster Meyer Lansky, and the Bugsy-Meyer mob stole cars for Lucky Luciano's men to drive during crimes and ran gambling and bootlegging rackets in the Tri-State area. Lansky and Siegel also did their share of raiding warehouses and hijacking trucks.

No one ever called Siegel "Bugsy" to his face. His friends called him Ben. Siegel was a hothead, who was always ready to solve disagreements by administering a beating. He also had no qualms about murder. Siegel was a professional—he always made sure to puncture his victims' stomachs with a long knife, so that when the victim started decomposing, the gas would escape through the puncture wounds and the body wouldn't float to the surface of the rivers where they were usually deposited. Siegel was known to have murdered mobsters Vincent "Mad Dog" Coll, Tony Fabrizzo, Waxey Gordon, Charles "Chink" Sherman, Bo Weinberg, Joey Amberg, Louis Amberg, Harry "Big Greenie" Greenberg, and Whitey Krakower. Only Siegel knew how many people he actually murdered.

Siegel was part of the hit team that whacked the old-school New York mafia dons Joe "The Boss" Masseria and Salvatore Maranzano in 1931. Getting rid of these two men ended the rule of the "Mustache Petes" and brought the mafia into the modern era. Known as "The Syndicate," the East Coast crime families agreed to coop-erate with each other and ex-pand their territories to Florida and the western states. Along with Lansky, Siegel co-founded Murder Inc., which supplied mob families with made-to-or-der hit men, ready to travel any-where to quietly kill enemies of the Syndicate. This was the greatest era of expansion for organized crime, and it would be thirty years before the U.S. Justice Department cracked down on the mob during the Kennedy administration.

The ever-dapper Benjamin "Bugsy" Siegel in 1941. *(Associated Press)*

Ironically, Siegel was a charming man who moved easily in high soci-ety. He was as comfortable with politicians and celebrities as he was with hookers and drug pushers. Siegel was the Syndicate's ambassador. He was the go-to guy used to grease the gears of city halls and zoning boards around the Eastern seaboard.

Siegel was a hands-on kind of mob boss. He loved working over a deadbeat or shooting a double-crosser. Eventually, though, he made too many enemies among various rival gangsters. In 1937, the Syndicate decided that it would be wise to send Bugsy to California to keep him out of harm's way and to shore up the rackets headed by Los Angeles crime boss Jack Dragna.

In California, Siegel set up a national wire service to connect Dragna's gambling dens and bookie parlors to the rest of the country. This scheme made enormous profits for the Syndicate. He also muscled in on Dragna's drug, extortion, and numbers rackets in Los Angeles. Because Siegel had the blessing of the Syndicate, Dragna had only two choices: comply or die. Dragna wisely complied.

Siegel rented a thirty-five-room mansion in Beverly Hills and looked up his childhood buddy, movie star George Raft. Raft introduced him to Hollywood royalty. Siegel's charm and fashion sense fit right in with the Hollywood crowd and he was soon hobnobbing with Clark Gable, Jean Harlow, Gary Cooper, and dozens of other show business fixtures. Siegel threw extravagant parties and bet as much as $10,000 a day at the Santa Anita racetrack, where he puzzlingly almost always won. He dated a string of starlets, even though he had moved his wife and children to Los Angeles.

Countess Dorothy Dendice Taylor diFrasso fell madly in love with Siegel and introduced him to movie moguls Jack Warner, Harry Cohn, and Louis B. Mayer. Siegel later extorted money from those producers and their studios. Later, on a trip to Italy, the countess allegedly introduced Siegel to Fascist dictator Benito Mussolini and Hitler henchmen Hermann Goering and Dr. Joseph Goebbels. Siegel was so disgusted by the Nazis that he allegedly had to be talked out of murdering them by the countess.

Through Virginia Hill, an aspiring starlet and mob money launderer, Siegel made Mexican connections and set up a heroin and opium smuggling operation that distributed dope throughout the United States. This action marked the beginning of the drug trade on the West Coast. Hill was the love of Siegel's sordid life. Although he was married and had constant affairs, he always returned to Hill's bed.

The laid-back West Coast atmosphere didn't change Siegel. He was still a hands-on mobster. He might go to a Hollywood premiere or go out nightclubbing with the stars, only to excuse himself to torture or kill an underworld figure who had fallen out of the graces of the Syndicate. Siegel made the most of his knowledge of the vices of the rich and famous, blackmailing them to keep their dirty laundry hidden.

Siegel financed a posh gambling ship, *The Rex*, which anchored twelve miles off the coast, just beyond the United States boundary. The success of this investment gave Siegel the idea of starting a casino in a small, dusty, desert hamlet—known by most people in Nevada as a lonely railroad tank town named Las Vegas.

Taking advantage of Nevada's lax gambling and prostitution laws, and using three million dollars of the Syndicate's money, Siegel built the Flamingo Hotel in the little town and, in essence, put Las Vegas on the map.

The first few months were rough for the Flamingo. Hordes of gamblers didn't flock out to the luxurious hotel right away, and the place was losing money. Siegel needed more money to promote his venture. He hired the biggest entertainers of the day, many who were repaying favors to Siegel, to perform at the Flamingo. His Hollywood pals followed suit, traveling to Las Vegas for nights of wild partying, making the once sleepy railroad town a fashionable place to be and be seen.

However, the money wasn't coming in fast enough for the Syndicate, and the boys back East felt like they had financed Siegel's personal playroom. Mob boss Lucky Luciano called Siegel to Havana, Cuba, where Luciano was secretly living after being deported from the United States, to demand his investment money back. Siegel was getting too big for his own good and, believing that he was an equal to the powerful Luciano, he told his old pal to "go to hell." In true Godfather fashion, Luciano didn't say a word and Siegel went back to the West Coast and to what he thought was his personal criminal fiefdom.

Benjamin "Bugsy" Siegel after he crossed his business partners. *(Associated Press)*

Luciano called Siegel's mentor and old business partner Meyer Lansky and informed him that it was time for Bugsy to go and there could be no discussion of the matter. Allegedly, Lansky called his old friend Bugsy and begged him to pay Luciano and apologize for his disrespect. Siegel ignored his old partner.

On June 20, 1947, Siegel was reading a newspaper in Virginia Hill's extravagant Beverly Hills home when someone fired three shots from a .30–30 rifle through a window, killing the mobster immediately. Hill was "vacationing" in Europe at the time and Bugsy's bodyguard just happened to leave the room before Siegel was shot.

Only Siegel's immediate family showed up for his funeral. His Hollywood friends, including George Raft, stayed away. The man who founded America's adult playground was put into his crypt, with a mere five people in attendance.

Interestingly, given the extremely small attendance at his internment, Bugsy's passing was not mourned by the California glitterati, whom he had used and abused for a decade.

Benjamin "Bugsy" Siegel gets a free ride in "the meat wagon." *(Associated Press)*

Chapter 29

The Last Lynching in California

Death Toll: 1

January 6, 1947, Callahan—Siskiyou County

For various, obvious reasons, lynching is a particularly heinous act. In the following case of the last known lynching in the state of California, a group of children also became unwilling victims of a terrible form of "justice."

The students arrived at the Callahan grade school in Siskiyou County, on a cold winter morning just as on any other winter school day. But January 6, 1947, was different. Strung up on the telephone pole in front of the school was the body of an African-American man with calfskin wrapped around his shoulders. Bullet holes could be seen on the bloodstained man.

All eight grades attended the same one-room school, and the children were ushered into the school by the teacher as the police and coroner's van arrived. An hour or so later, a young boy went outside to use the outhouse and bumped into a tall man wearing a suit and a cowboy hat. The first grader asked the man what had happened. "That's to teach you kids what happens when you rustle cattle," he replied.

Callahan was literally a cowtown when the last known lynching in California took place. *(California State Library Photograph Collection)*

The teacher of Callahan school later told her pupils, "You are never again to talk about what happened here today."

The Callahan grade school in Sis-kiyou County where on January 6, 1947, an unidentified African-American was strung up on a telephone pole and shot. *(California State Library Photograph Collection)*

On Friday, January 10, 1947, the *Western Sentinel* newspaper carried a front-page story about the lynching of the African-American butcher from Weed, California. A few days later, the *Etna Gazette* carried the story about a butcher who was lynched after being caught stealing a calf. Soon afterwards, all the copies of the Sunday, January 12, 1947, issue of the *Etna Gazette* and all the copies of the January 10 issue of the *Western Sentinel* disappeared, including the Siskiyou County library's copy, and so details of this lynching are scarce.

What we do know is that in the early morning hours of January 6, 1947, near Gazelle in southern Siskiyou County, a small mob of local ranchers shot, wounded, and captured a sus-pected cattle rustler on a ranch owned by a well-known Yreka medical doctor. From there, the man was taken to the village of Callahan and hanged from the utility pole in front of Callahan's one-room schoolhouse. A cover-up was arranged by the so-called respected citizens of Gazelle, who with the help of local authorities managed to re-move all documented evidence concerning the lynching. Chances are good that at the time of this writing, some of the people involved are still alive and living in the area.

It was the last known lynching in California.

Lynch-mob participants were seldom brought to justice themselves, so it is not surprising that the citizens of Gazelle and Callahan were able to carry off a total cover-up the lynching of this man, whose name has been lost to history.

Chapter 30

Shootout at the Supper Club

Death Toll: 1

February 15, 1962, Sacramento—Sacramento County

It is always tragic when valiant officers of the law are killed in the line of duty. However, the price paid for public safety is often high and the selfless risks taken by lawmen certainly become a reward of their own nature.

On the night of February 15, 1962, Aaron Charles Mitchell walked unnoticed through the kitchen door of the Stadium Club in Sacramento's south side. Wearing rubber gloves and a homemade ski mask, Mitchell obviously wasn't at the restaurant to make a delivery.

Bursting into the bar and dining room, Mitchell fired a round into the ceiling from the sawed-off shotgun that he had tied around his neck. He got everyone's immediate attention. He held thirty patrons and employees at gunpoint and mumbled something about someone opening the safe. However, he settled for two hundred dollars taken from co-owner Jack Licciardo's wallet.

Unknown to Mitchell, Jack's brother and co-owner Edward had slipped into another room and phoned the police. Officers John Bibica, Robert Reese, Arnold Gamble, and Ronald Shaw arrived in minutes. Bibica covered the front door, while Reese, Gamble, and Shaw entered through the back door.

Mitchell looked around at the angry patrons of the supper club and realized that he was in over his head, and there was no way that he could have ever pulled off the heist alone. He backed his way toward the front entrance to make an exit.

Seeing Officer Bibica covering the entrance, Mitchell turned and ran through the kitchen just as Officer Shaw was entering. Mitchell stuck his shotgun into Officer Shaw's face and took his gun. He grabbed Shaw and shoved him through the door, using him as a shield. Mitchell fired Shaw's pistol four times, hitting Officer Gamble in the chest and killing him, but not before the brave policeman fired his high-powered revolver four times. Officer Shaw was hit in the left thigh. Officer Reese was forced to hold his fire because officers Gamble and Shaw were in his line of fire.

Hearing the shots, Officer Bibica ran around to the back of the restaurant and saw Mitchell run through the parking lot, across the street, and into a field of tall grass. Bibica fired five shots at Mitchell, saving his last shot. Officer Reese was also hot on Mitchell's trail, firing off several rounds at the fleeing murderer. The lawmen followed Mitchell's bloody path, which led to a guest house a few blocks away from the Stadium Club.

Joined by Officer Jerry Finney, and with their guns reloaded, the policemen kicked in the guest house door, where they found Mitchell lying wounded and unconscious on his back, his shotgun still tied around his neck and lying across his chest. He was still wearing his rubber gloves and mask. He had been shot five times. His getaway car was located nearby.

Officer Gamble would have been forty-three years old on the day after he died. His wife of twenty-four years, two children, and a grandchild survived him.

Aaron Charles Mitchell had been out on bond in connection with a robbery of the Norge Laundry and Dry Cleaning Village on December 29, 1961. He had been arrested in five different states for robbery and grand larceny and had twice served time in prison. He may have also been responsible for several other Sacramento robberies. After a six-week trial, Mitchell was sentenced to death.

> *Career criminal Charles Mitchell finally pulled a job that was too big for his capabilities. While his attempt to bail out was futile, his actions cost the life of a man whose contributions to society were so much greater than his own.*

Chapter 31

Sirhan Sirhan and the Whispering Woman in the Polka Dot Dress

Death Toll: 1

June 5, 1968, Los Angeles—Los Angeles County

By the time of the Robert F. Kennedy assassination, lynchings, thankfully, were a "thing of the past." However, when evidence is cloudy, motive uncertain, and conspiracy theories abound, even well deserved verdicts are handed down by fallible jury members, and both the public and the workings of the justice system may well remain unsatisfied.

The 1968 presidential race turned into an open ticket for both the Republican and Democratic parties after President Lyndon Johnson, who was John F. Kennedy's vice president and became the "Leader of the Free World" after President Kennedy was assassinated in Dallas in 1963, decided not to run for reelection. After winning the 1964 Presidential election and pushing through the long-overdue Civil Rights Act of 1964, Johnson felt hamstrung by the American involvement in Vietnam, which he had escalated, and this led to his belief that he would not be able to govern properly.

Robert Kennedy was President Kennedy's younger brother. Besides being his brother's most trusted advisor, Bobby served in his brother's administration as attorney general. After his brother's assassination, he became a U.S. senator from New York. When President Johnson decided not to run for reelection, the opportunity to win the Democratic Party's nomination for president was too great for Kennedy to resist. He threw his hat into the ring.

Kennedy had to win the California primary election, both for the sake of his own campaign and for the unity of the Democratic Party. Only a week before the California primary, he had lost the Oregon primary to Minnesota Senator Eugene McCarthy, who had motivated America's youth with his anti-war platform. California had 174 delegates, and the bustling population of college students and other draft-age voters working against

Robert F. Kennedy accepts victory in the 1968 California Democratic presidential primary at a speech in the Ambassador Hotel in Los Angeles. Minutes after this photo was taken, R.F.K. was assassinated. *(Associated Press)*

him made it crucial for Kennedy to win in order stymie McCarthy's momentum. Bombastic debates over policies were the last thing that the Democratic Party wanted at their convention. Republican Richard Nixon was leading the Republican ticket with his conservative message and pro-Vietnam War stance. The Democratic Party could not win the presidential election if its party was divided.

On June 4, 1968, more than two thousand Kennedy supporters celebrated in the Embassy Ballroom in Los Angeles's Ambassador Hotel as the election results came in. Kennedy had won California.

Security was almost non-existent for Kennedy, although the Ambassador Hotel had boosted its security staff with a few hired guards from Ace Security, a local protection firm. Kennedy had a huge entourage of aides, advisors, relatives, and show business personalities that followed him everywhere. His personal bodyguards were football great Roosevelt "Rosey" Grier and 1960 Olympic decathlon champ Rafer Johnson.

After giving a rousing victory speech, Kennedy began to make his way from the hotel. The route took him through the narrow pantry of the ballroom's kitchen. Surrounded by his entourage, Kennedy moved slowly through the crowd, shaking hands with well-wishers. As he was being led by the arm by Ace Security guard Thane Eugene Cesar, a slightly built Palestinian immigrant named Sirhan Bishara Sirhan walked up to Kennedy and shot him behind the right ear with a .22 caliber Iver-Johnson eight-cylinder revolver, a Mafia-style shooting.

Pandemonium broke out. Writer George Plimpton, Grier, Johnson, and California state assembly member Jesse Unruh jumped on the assassin and pinned him to a steam table, as Sirhan emptied his gun into the crowd. Sirhan was freakishly strong, able to struggle with the four strong men while continuing to fire, hitting Kennedy two more times under his right armpit.

Hit in the head were speech writer Paul Schrade and artist and Kennedy friend Elizabeth Evans. ABC-TV director William Weisel was shot in the stomach; reporter Ira Goldstein was hit in the hip; and seven-year-old Irwin Stroll was grazed in the kneecap.

Kennedy lay sprawled on the tile floor, blood pouring from his wounds. He was taken first to Central Receiving Hospital, but was quickly sent to Good Samaritan Hospital, where neurosurgeons were on duty. The doctors worked frantically on Kennedy, doing what they could.

A squad of police officers formed a flying wedge, rushing Sirhan through the crowded ballroom, where word had spread that Kennedy had been shot, and out of the hotel. The crowd was obviously hostile to Sirhan, spitting on him and jeering him. In another era, he would have been lynched, but police did not want to see a repeat of what had happened in Dallas with Lee Harvey Oswald, who had shot President Kennedy and was in turn assassinated by nightclub owner Jack Ruby.

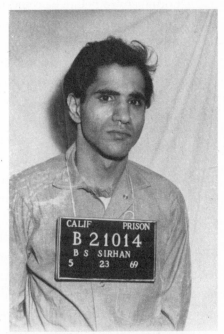

Robert F. Kennedy died the next day of his wounds, and the nation mourned. The assassination likely changed the course of history, as Richard Nixon defeated Democratic nominee Hubert Humphrey in an extremely close race. Humphrey won the popular vote, but Nixon won the majority of electoral votes.

Police searched Sirhan's Pasadena home and discovered evidence that incriminated Sirhan but did

Sirhan Sirhan, killer of Robert F. Kennedy or hypnotized patsy? *(Associated Press)*

little to explain his motive. Sirhan's family were Palestinian Christians who had moved to the United States when Sirhan was four years old. His abusive father could not adjust to American culture and moved back to Israel, leaving his wife and family to fend for themselves.

Sirhan had led a fairly normal life, working low-paying jobs and attending some college classes. While working as a groomer at the Santa Anita racetrack, he was thrown from a horse and suffered a head injury. People who knew him said he was never the same after the accident.

Sirhan became involved with several religions—Baptist, Seventh Day Adventist, and a few obscure cults—and he supported Iraq's Baath Party. Still, there appeared to be no real rationale for Sirhan to throw away his life to assassinate Kennedy.

Two witnesses told police that shortly before the shooting, they saw Sirhan whispering to a man and to a woman, who had a "pug" nose and who wore a white dress with black or blue polka dots. As he arrived at the hotel, LAPD sergeant Paul Sharaga reported he had overheard a woman wearing a polka dot dress say, "We shot Kennedy." However, she was lost in the exiting crowd before he could react. Some speculated that the lady in the polka dot dress might have hypnotized Sirhan. Police discounted the theory.

Sirhan pleaded not guilty at this trial, changed his plea, and then pleaded guilty. "Just execute me!" he pleaded to the judge. He claimed he could not remember a thing about the entire night of the shooting, and he informed the court that he had been intoxicated. He told the judge that he might have become temporarily insane over Kennedy's support of Israel.

After three days of deliberation, the jury found Sirhan guilty of the first-degree murder of Senator Robert F. Kennedy and five counts of assault with a deadly weapon. He was sentenced to life in prison and taken to Corcoran State Prison.

As in the assassination of his brother before him, conspiracy theories were rampant concerning the assassination of Robert F. Kennedy. Kennedy had made many enemies while he was attorney general, especially the organized crime mobster Sam "Momo" Giancana. Kennedy had also been responsible for the imprisonment of Teamsters president Jimmy Hoffa.

There is also the mystery of the possibility of a second shooter. Powder burns around Kennedy's head wound indicated that the fatal shot was fired from a distance of a few inches. Sirhan Sirhan was never, at any time, that close to Kennedy. Los Angeles County Coroner Thomas Noguchi stated that there were two bullet holes in the door jamb near where Kennedy was gunned down, and the door frame was disassembled and taken to LAPD crime lab for tests. After x-raying the wood, the LAPD concluded that the bullet-pocked pantry was not important and destroyed it before Sirhan was brought to trial. Assistant Police Chief Daryl Gates, who later was chief of police of the Los Angeles Police Department during the Rodney King incident and riots that followed, was the lead investigator.

With all the seedy characters involved directly and indirectly in the assassination of Robert Kennedy, we will likely never know what truly happened on that June evening.

Both John F. Kennedy and his brother Robert F. Kennedy were assassinated by highly unstable individuals. This is certain. What is not certain is whether the actions of the assassins were part of a larger conspiracy, or whether Oswald and Sirhan had accomplices. While the debates and uncertainties concerning these two tragic assassinations will likely never abate, surely Oswald and Sirhan paid their respective dues for their roles in the murders.

Chapter 32

The Golden Dragon Massacre

Death Toll: 5 Wounded: 11

September 5, 1977, Chinatown, San Francisco—San Francisco County

By the last quarter of the twentieth century, gang violence had become endemic in urban areas of California, although Chinese gangs had been a pestilence in San Francisco for over a century.

"It was just like we went to a movie last night. Only it was real…"

A large and boisterous crowd of seventy-five people sat eating a late dinner at the Golden Dragon, a popular Chinese restaurant in San Francisco's Chinatown. At 2:40 A.M. on September 5, 1977, three masked men burst through the glass double doors at the eatery and sprayed gunfire at the patrons. The assailants ignored a nearby cash register and never uttered a word during the one minute they were inside. One of the shooters carried a shotgun, which he used to blast at tables at point-blank range. Another man had a .38-caliber pistol, while the third toted a .45-caliber Thompson submachine gun that he sprayed from one end of the room to the other.

It was the worst mass slaying in San Francisco's history. When police arrived, the scene looked like the aftermath of a firefight in Vietnam; bodies and blood were spewed everywhere and people were screaming and moaning. Five people died and eleven were wounded.

The gunmen vanished before anybody could get a good enough look at them to provide a clear description. Due to the indiscriminate nature of the attack and the wild firing of the assailants, the dead and wounded lay in varied locations throughout the restaurant. One woman had been riddled with machine gun fire from head to toe, but she clung to life and would survive. Another man lay on the floor with a large hole in his chest; he also recovered. The wounds were so grave that it would take over one hundred pints of blood to save the wounded after they were transported to San Francisco General Hospital.

Given the wild and indiscriminate shooting, it was a miracle that more people were not killed that night. Among the dead was a forty-eight-year-old waiter and father of eight, Fong Wong. He had been unlucky enough to be standing near the entrance and was shot in the neck. Twenty-year-old Donald Kwan and eighteen-year-old Riordan High School honor student Calvin Michael Fong had been hit by a shotgun blast as they sat with three friends. Twenty-year-old Seattle tourist Denise Louie and twenty-five-year-old law student Paul Wada also were killed. Wada was shot nine times, and this initially gave rise to the theory that he was the main target. Mayor George Moscone, who ironically would be assassinated within the next year, issued a $25,000 reward for information leading to the capture of the killers. The Golden Dragon reopened for business the same day, after the bloodstained walls and carpet were hurriedly cleaned.

The San Francisco Police Department immediately speculated the killings were somehow gang-related. Since 1970, thirty-nine people of Chinese heritage had been killed during drive-by shootings and assassinations. The United States ended national quotas against Chinese immigration in 1965 and hundreds of thousands of new immigrants from China soon landed on U.S. shores. In the late 1960s and early 1970s, California welcomed thousands of them. As with all populations of impoverished immigrants, some of the immigrants became gang members and created a new colony of Chinese gangs in California. This didn't sit well with the American-born Chinese, who had had their own gang affiliations, called "tongs," in San Francisco since the city was established. The foreign-born Chinese battled over the control of turf, the right to receive protection money from Chinese businesses, and the proceeds from fireworks and gambling rackets. The homicide rate within the Chinese community of San Francisco skyrocketed.

In 1973, seventeen-year-old Philip Kyee was shot to death in front of the Golden Dragon restaurant after an argument inside the establishment.

Yet, the Chinese community remained relatively silent after this attack, when questioned by police. They naturally feared reprisals from the Chinese gangs who had terrorized San Francisco for a century. However, none of the dead or wounded from the Golden Dragon massacre turned out to be a gang member.

Police investigations subsequently revealed that the assassins were part of the Joe Fong gang, also known as Joe's Boys. The three triggermen were discovered to be Curtis Tam, Melvin Yu, and Peter Ng. Another gang member, Tom Yu, planned the attack but did not directly take part in the shootings. He accidentally admitted to his involvement in the killings after being audiotaped by a Chinese undercover police officer, and he was arrested in March 1978. Tam, who had migrated to San Francisco with his parents from Hong Kong in 1976, claimed to have participated in the murders only under duress. He confessed and implicated the other trigger men.

A year to the day after the shootings, Judge Calcagno announced the guilty verdict for all four men. The methodology of the gunmen indicated that, while the event was gang-related, it was not carried out professionally. The masks the men were wearing (two wore ski masks; the other wore a Halloween mask) betrayed the fact that they were Asian and Chinese to bystanders. The men entered the restaurant with their guns drawn and fired at the ceiling first, giving time for their real targets, the rival Wah Ching (Chinese Youth) gang leader Michael "Hot Dog" Louie and his henchmen, to respond. One of the clear-eyed gang members had shouted to Louie, "Man with a gun," giving Louie time to get to safety under a table. The rest of the Wah Ching gang stuck their faces to the floor. None received gunshot wounds. The innocent bystanders who were seated and standing next to the gang members were the unfortunate victims of the attack. Many ran in panic, only to be cut down by the ruthless and wild-eyed men in this senseless act of murder.

Ironically, none of the intended gang-member targets were killed or wounded during the Golden Dragon massacre, and, tragically, all of the victims were innocent bystanders. Happily, in this case, the perpetrators were eventually nailed by the authorities. However, the California citizenry and the California legal system have continued to be plagued by increasing gang violence until the present time.

Chapter 33

Warfare at City Hall

Death Toll: 3

November 27, 1978, San Francisco—San Francisco County

Although not unknown in the annals of California history, it is rare when those elected as defenders of the public interest themselves become perpetrators or victims of murderous violence. However, San Francisco city politics was chaotic during the late 1970s, and a volcano was about to erupt at city hall.

In 1976, George Richard Moscone was sitting on the top of the world. At age forty-seven, he had become the mayor of San Francisco. Not bad for a poor native son from a broken home. Little did Moscone know that he and city supervisor Harvey Milk would be assassinated in his office at city hall in two years by disgruntled former city supervisor Dan White.

The mayor was born in San Francisco on November 24, 1929, to George and Lena Moscone. His father was a milkman who spent most of his paycheck on the night life that San Francisco is so famous for. The marriage broke up when young George was eight years old. Lena was a secretary and worked at a liquor store on the weekends. The elder George bounced from job to job, even working in San Quentin Prison for a while, but eventually he went mad and was interned in a state mental hospital.

With the guidance of their Catholic faith, young George and his mother persevered and prospered. George graduated from Saint Ignatius High School, attended Santa Rosa Junior College, and then transferred to the University of the Pacific. His steel-trap mind put him through Hastings

San Francisco Supervisor Harvey Milk and Mayor George Moscone entertain the press after signing the city's gay rights bill. *(Associated Press)*

School of Law, where he befriended another future mayor of the "City By the Bay," Willie Brown.

Moscone was a lifelong ladies' man; nevertheless, he married Gina Bodanza and had four children. The California Democratic Party noticed the charisma that the handsome young lawyer oozed and asked him to run for a seat in the state assembly. He lost the first time, but eventually won a San Francisco senate seat in the legislature at Sacramento. Subsequently, Moscone rose up the political ladder, becoming a San Francisco city supervisor and, ultimately, mayor of San Francisco.

Moscone always sided with the dockworkers, sailors, shoprats, seamstresses, nurses, prostitutes, and teachers who had built his beloved city, rather than with the masters of industry, real estate moguls, and members of the downtown financial core. He once gave his barber the key to the city. Needless to say, Moscone made some enemies with the powerful elite of San Francisco.

Dan White was a straight-laced all-American fellow from the once-Irish, working class Southside Valley neighborhood of Excelsior. A former Marine sergeant and Vietnam veteran, who later admitted that he had never fired his weapon at anyone the entire time he was in Vietnam, White joined the San Francisco Police Department after he was honorably discharged in 1969. After a few years, he quit the police force to join the San Francisco Fire Department. Like most young men, he drank with the guys and played the field, dating numerous women, although none of these relationships was serious until he met Mary Ann Burns, whom he married.

White was thrust into politics with the help of former supervisor John Barbagelata. Barbagelata narrowly lost the mayor's race to George Moscone in the brutal 1975 elections. During their televised debate, Barbagelata refused to shake Moscone's hand, and he declared that Moscone was a "bad" Catholic.

Following the 1975 mayoral election, Barbagelata kept his supervisor's position, where he opposed many of Moscone's programs. In 1977, Barbagelata mounted a failed recall campaign against Moscone. When San Francisco's board of supervisors was split into eleven neighborhood supervisory districts due to a 1975 city initiative, Barbagelata realized that his pro-downtown, pro-business power base would be lost, and he decided against running for reelection. The clean-cut White would be a perfect puppet.

White was naïve about life in general. He believed that as long as he had his books and a mattress, he'd be all right, even though he had a wife and child. After his election as supervisor, White was required by city law to quit his job at the fire department. He had a hard time realizing that he could not support his family on the $10,000-a-year supervisor's salary. His new downtown elite "friends" set him up with a baked potato stand at Fisherman's Wharf.

White did not know how to play politics. He would promise Moscone or Milk to support a proposal and then vote against it during the actual ballot. White once pitched the idea of having the board of supervisors start a softball team, an idea that was laughed out of the council chamber.

Harvey Milk was born on May 22, 1930, in Long Island, New York, and saddled with the nickname Glimpy Milch, Milch being the Lithuanian surname of his grandfather and Glimpy a commentary on his awkward appearance. After he graduated from Albany State College in 1951, Milk joined the navy but he was later dishonorably discharged for being gay.

With its numerous navy bases, San Francisco is a major terminus for sailors mustering out. Many gay sailors stayed in San Francisco after they were discharged because of its Bohemian nightlife and tolerance toward homosexuals. The sailors who were dishonorably discharged because of their homosexuality also found that it was preferable to stay in San Francisco than to go back to their homes and explain to their family and friends why their naval careers had ended less than honorably.

Milk moved to San Francisco in 1972 with his boyfriend, Scott Smith, and opened a camera store in the Castro District. He quickly rose as a community leader and founded the Castro Valley Association of Local Merchants. He represented the neighborhood businesses in their dealings with the city government.

Mayor Moscone's policies began to make San Francisco's old-line police officers edgy. They were used to drinking while on duty and beating up gays and minorities. Some of the city's minority police officers were suing the department for discrimination in hiring and promoting, and Mayor Moscone championed their cause, offering the wronged officers an out-of-court settlement. This infuriated the old-guard police and firemen. The police felt that Moscone had betrayed them. Over the years, they had looked the other way while the mayor allegedly dallied with prostitutes. There was talk of assassinating the mayor among the very people who were hired to stop crime. Moscone also angered the police by hiring an outsider, former Oakland police chief Charles Gain, as the new San Francisco chief of police. Gain angered the rank and file even further when he had all the city's police cars painted powder blue.

The Sisters of the Good Shepherd wanted to build a youth campus for mentally disturbed adolescent San Franciscans in District Eight. The idea was to keep them close to friends and family and in the city where they lived, instead of sending them to the state hospital in Napa. Dan White was against having the institution in his district and sought Harvey Milk's vote against it, promising Milk his vote for the nation's first gay rights law that was coming up on the San Francisco board of supervisors agenda. Milk voted for the gay rights bill, but he also voted for the youth campus. White lost the vote and the campus was built in District Eight.

White became increasingly frustrated with politics. He dreaded going to the Monday night board meetings. His desk at his office was generally empty and White was rarely seen at city hall. He stopped caring about what his handlers and constituents wanted.

White finally resigned from the board of supervisors on November

10, 1978. Mayor Moscone didn't want to accept the resignation, but once word got out, board clerk Gil Boreman went up to the mayor's office, got a copy of the letter, and took it down to his chamber, where he stamped it with the seal of the city, making the resignation offical.

The residents of District Eight were furious. Neighborhood activists, led by White's onetime campaign manager Goldie Judge, held a rally accusing White of being a pawn of the Police Officers Association and the chamber of commerce. White showed up at the rally and words were exchanged, all in front of television news cameras.

White decided that he didn't want to resign after all. He informed the mayor of his wishes, but Moscone was advised by other members of the board of supervisors not to let White back on the board.

Tragedy struck San Francisco on November 18, 1978, when California congressman Leo Ryan flew with some staff members and reporters to inspect former San Franciscan Jim Jones's People's Temple compound in Guyana. Relatives of Jones's followers had asked the congressman to check out what was happening to loved ones who had moved with Jones to the tiny South American country. All was not well at Jonestown, where Jones's devotees were virtual slaves. As Ryan and his entourage were getting on their plane to head back to the U.S., they were ambushed and killed by Jones's goon squad of murderers. Jones then had his members drink

Harvey Milk, Mayor George Moscone, and their assassin, Dan White. *(Associated Press)*

poisioned fruit juice and commit mass suicide. Over seven hundred people, most of them from San Francisco, died in the hot tropical sun.

The mass suicide embarrassed Moscone, as he had once named the Reverend Jim Jones to head up San Francisco's housing authority. He knew that the disaster would provide his opposition with political fodder during his reelection campaign.

White learned from the media that the mayor was not planning to allow him back on the board of supervisors. Local reporters ripped White to shreds in the newspapers and on radio and television. Dan White's political career was completely destroyed.

White couldn't sleep on the night of November 26, 1978. He paced the floor of his home all night, eating cupcakes. In the morning, he loaded his .38 with hollow-point bullets and dumped six more into his pocket. He put on a shoulder holster, slipped his revolver into it, and put on a jacket to hide it. An aide unwittingly drove him to city hall, where White said he was going to ask the mayor for his job back.

Instead of walking through the main entrance where metal detectors were installed, White climbed through an open basement window. He identified himself to the occupants of the room, telling the engineer that he had lost his key.

At the mayor's office, Moscone's secretary let White in to see the mayor. In Moscone's office, White demanded his job back. Moscone told him that it wasn't going to happen. He offered White a drink. White asked again for his job back but the answer was still no. White pulled out his pistol and stuck it into Moscone's chest, firing twice. The mayor fell face down onto the floor. White pumped two more shots into the back of the mayor's head.

White reloaded his gun and walked over to Harvey Milk's office. Supervisor Dianne Feinstein saw him walk by and called out to him. White ignored her.

Finding Supervisor Milk in his office, White began yelling at him. Milk smiled at White, who then pulled out his gun and shot Milk in the stomach and chest. Milk tried to get away, but White fired a round into his back and another into the back of his head. He then fired a final round point-blank into Milk's head.

As the murderer escaped down a stairway, he passed a city worker he knew and cheerily greeted her. He got into his aide's car and they drove away, the aide apparently unaware of the crimes that Supervisor Dan White had just committed.

White called his wife and had her meet him at Saint Mary's Cathedral. He told her, "I shot the mayor and Harvey." White then turned himself in at the North Station a short time later.

The San Francisco police took good care of the murderer. They brought him meals from restaurants, allowed visitors, and made sure that nobody harmed him. An organization called "The Friends of Dan White" was put together to make sure that White's wife, Mary Ann, would not be troubled financially.

After a lengthy jury trial, Dan White was convicted of voluntary manslaughter. His lawyers blamed White's depression and junk food addition for his violent act. He received only a five-to-seven year sentence in prison for the assassinations of two government officials. Mobs formed in the Castro District as the news spread. People poured out of the bars and onto Market Street. A huge mob of angry protesters moved on city hall. The police were completely taken by surprise by the violent crowd. They were used to slapping gays around without retribution. However, the gay community in San Francisco had had enough of being bullied by the police and a full-blown riot broke out. The mob trashed dozens of police cars, broke windows in the city hall, and nailed acting Mayor Dianne Feinstein in the head with a rock when she came out onto the stairs of city hall to ask the rioters to cease their protest. For hours, protesters fought in hand-to-hand combat with the outnumbered police.

Later that night, San Francisco's "finest" committed their own twisted version of payback, by taking off their badges and raiding a popular drinking establishment called the Elephant Walk, beating the patrons and employees with their batons. The city's gay population quickly organized and counter-attacked the rogue police officers, and the police fled.

Dan White was sent to Soledad Prison, south of the Bay Area, where he was put into a protective cellblock reserved for celebrity criminals and snitches. He became friends with Robert F. Kennedy's assassin, Sirhan Sirhan.

White was paroled in 1984 and moved to a Los Angeles-area halfway house. After a year of probation, Dan White was free to go anywhere he chose, but Mayor Feinstein asked him not to come back to his hometown of San Francisco. He ignored her pleas and moved back to his old neighborhood.

On October 21, 1985, Dan White commited suicide by running a hose from the exhaust pipe of his yellow 1979 Buick LeSabre into the passenger compartment. He died of carbon monoxide poisoning.

To memorialize Mayor Moscone, the city renamed the Yerba Buena Center, San Francisco's convention center, as the Moscone Center. Ironically, Mayor Moscone had been passionately opposed to the construction of the center, as it destroyed an entire working-class neighborhood.

Dan White's cold-blooded murder of Mayor Moscone and Supervisor Milk supercharged emotions in the San Francisco gay community and caused a violent riot. Had the events occurred a century earlier, they would almost certainly have led to a lynching. While White's sentence appeared lenient, he would later inflict a much harsher penalty upon himself.

Chapter 34

Psychopaths Carry Out Some Bank Business

Death Toll: 2

February 28, 1997, North Hollywood—Los Angeles County

Hollywood has a long tradition of making movies that glamorize violence, shootouts, robberies, and the ongoing war between law enforcement officers and badmen. In the following case, two misfits were unduly influenced by this Hollywood tradition, and horrific violence was the result.

Everybody has seen ridiculously long shootouts in films and on television, where two men take on dozens of black-swathed fighters, making impossible shots and taking bullets dozens of times without even breaking a sweat. The men are courageous, good-looking, and honorable. The violence spills out onto the streets for blocks, cars crash, fire hydrants burst, and fruit stands get overturned. In reality, the average criminal shootout lasts mere seconds. The criminals are scared (and not at all good-looking) and shoot wildly, and their odds are not too good. A real shootout can only end in one of three ways: win, escape, or die. The latter is the typical outcome. The police are highly trained in gun skills and have to practice and pass firing tests on a regular basis. Most criminals are poor shots. And, in some cases, like the Golden Dragon massacre in San Francisco, criminals don't even know the fundamentals of operating a firearm.

Social misfits, Larry Eugene Phillips, Jr. and Emil Dechebal Matasareanu were not average criminals. While they knew how to operate automatic weapons, they were ignorant in the techniques of robbing banks.

The golden rule of robbing a bank is the "two-minute rule"—you must be in and out of the bank within two minutes. Pioneered by master bank robber Hermann "Baron" Lamm in the 1920s, the two-minute rule is the average time it takes for police to respond to a bank alarm. Lamm would carry a stopwatch to his robberies and have a cohort call out the seconds. Lamm would build mock-ups of the interior of the bank he was planning to rob, and his men would practice knocking it over. Lamm was killed on December 16, 1930, in Clinton, Indiana, while attempting to escape a heist gone wrong. But Matasareanu and Phillips would linger at their heists from six to eight minutes! An eternity in bank-robbing time.

Larry Eugene Phillips, Jr. was born under the name Larry Warfel. His father, Larry, was a two-bit criminal who blamed his hard-luck life on the police, federal agents, and anyone else in a uniform. He taught little Larry to hate the police. Law enforcement gave him plenty of help, once arresting him in front of thirteen-year-old junior for running a counterfeiting ring.

Young Larry was smart, but he dropped out of school after ninth grade and bounced between Denver and Los Angeles until his early twenties. He began weightlifting and wanted to get into competition, but he didn't have the grace or good looks necessary to become the next Arnold Schwarzenegger. Phillips dreamed of being rich, but he didn't want to earn his money through hard work. He wanted to obtain wealth the easy way, just like his dear old dad. He studied real estate and passed the state real estate exam, but was denied a license because he had a criminal record for stealing $400 worth of suits from Sears. Ironically, he had stolen the suits so he'd look like a respectable real estate agent.

Not being licensed as a real estate agent didn't stop Phillips. He started a shell company called Capital West Investments and sold counterfeit second mortgages without the property owners' knowledge. While working the scheme in Orange County, he was eventually busted. A civil judgment went against him, but he never paid the judgment amount. Philips fled to Colorado and began renting out vacant apartments and condos, again without the true owners' knowledge. He'd pocket the deposit and first month's rent. He was busted again, made bail, went on the lam (yes, sort of like the same Lamm who invented the two-minute rule), and fled back to south-

A heavily armored and armed Larry Eugene Phillips, Jr. taunts the L.A.P.D. with automatic weapon fire after a bungled bank robbery in North Hollywood. *(Associated Press)*

ern California, leaving behind his girlfriend and their two young children, who never saw Phillips again.

Phillips took up with an old childhood friend, Jeanette Federico, and lived with her and her child in the Los Angeles area under an alias. It was during this time that Phillips met Emil Dechebal Matasareanu.

Matasareanu was born in communist Romania, but he defected while on tour in Italy with his mother, an opera singer, and his father. They ended up in the Los Angeles area where they started a residential board-and-care facility for mentally disabled young adults. The state of California paid Emil's mother $2,000 a month per patient.

Matasareanu was chronically overweight and he became a social misfit who had no friends. He worked at the boarding home and got a degree in computer programming from DeVry Institute. He tried starting a business, but his lack of social skills with which to charm potential customers caused his business effort to fall flat. So, Matasareanu continued to work at his mother's facility, which was encountering problems with state inspectors, who eventually closed the place down.

Matasareanu married a Romanian girl and brought her back to America to live with his mother and the developmentally disabled lodgers. He gradually became increasingly paranoid and started acting violent, threatening neighbors and shaking patients. To fight his battle with obesity, Matasareanu started working out at a Gold's Gym in Venice, where he met his soon-to-be partner in crime, Larry Eugene Phillips, Jr.

The two misfits were like two peas in a pod. They both had undergone bizarre upbringings, they were both failures at everything they attempted, and they both had wives and kids. They played video games together and dreamed of being mercenaries or hit men. As they cleaned their guns together, they fed off each other's resentment of authority. The pair finally decided to commit armed robbery in order to achieve the American Dream.

They went to Littleton, Colorado, in 1993 to pull off their first heist. Phillips knew the area well and he knew he could be back in L.A. in a little more than a day. Wearing theatrical makeup to look older, the partners waited for a Wells Fargo armored truck to make a delivery. Instead of robbing the runner on his way into the bank, loaded with fresh bills worth $192,000, they waited for the runner to come out of the bank where they robbed him at gunpoint. They got away with $23,000 worth of worn and mutilated bills that the bank was returning to the Federal Reserve.

Back in southern California after spending their money, Phillips and Matasareanu were pulled over by a Glendale police officer. Phillips didn't have a license or registration for his car, and since he had no charisma whatsoever, he was soon on the hood of the police car, handcuffed, along with his buddy Matasareanu. While searching Phillips's red Thunderbird, police found a .45 caliber pistol, MAC-90 and AK-47 assault rifles, two black ski masks, body armor, police scanners, extra California license plates, smoke grenades, theatrical makeup, and a couple of thousand rounds of ammunition. Matasareanu pleaded to a weapons charge and received a sentence of seventy-one days in jail and three years probation. Phillips was sentenced to three years probation and ninety-nine days in jail. While in the slammer, Phillips married Jeanette Federico, who was nine months pregnant with their son. Incredibly, after Philips and Matasareanu had finished their time, most of their weapons were returned to them.

On June 14, 1995, Matasareanu and Phillips crouched behind a four-foot-tall concrete wall, waiting for a Brinks armored car to roll up to the Bank of America branch on Roscoe Boulevard in Canoga Park. As the fifty-one-year-old guard, Herman Dwight Cook, opened the side door holding a bag of money from the bank, Matasareanu and Phillips opened up on him with their AK-47s. The armor-piercing rounds went through Cook's bulletproof vest, killing him where he stood. Phillips grabbed the money, while Matasareanu fired at the driver. They made off with $122,000, driving a stolen white Chevrolet Celebrity.

Bank robbery is a federal crime, which places it under the Federal Bureau of Investigation's jurisdiction. However, Los Angeles is the bank robbery capital of the world, and so the FBI works closely with the Los Angeles Police Department. Both agencies were shocked by the holdup. Phillips and Matasareanu didn't even yell "Hands up" to Cook before they gunned him down in cold blood. And, they committed the crime in broad daylight in front of a gas station as if they didn't care if they were caught. Matasareanu even looked over at the people filling their tanks and told them to "Get down and don't look," before he went back to firing his rifle at the cab of the armored car. Witnesses said that the robbers moved slowly, like they had all the time in the world. Because of their use of heavy-duty weapons and body armor, the cops believed that the unknown men were right-wing terrorists.

Herman Dwight Cook, the guard who was slaughtered, had worked for Brinks for five years. It was to be a stop-gap job after he had been laid off by an aerospace firm. He was a husband and father of two, just trying to get by. That fatal day was the only time he ever faced a robbery.

On March 27, 1996, Phillips and Matasareanu decided to rob another armored car. At 9:30 A.M., they drove a stolen red Ford Econoline van head-on into the path of a Brinks truck on Fallbrook Avenue in the San Fernando Valley. One of the duo hung out of the passenger-side window, firing an AK-47. Three of the armor-piercing bullets went through the windshield, slightly wounding the Brinks driver, who wisely kept driving. The red van turned around and chased the Brinks truck for a few blocks before breaking away. The van was later found, engulfed in flames.

The FBI and the LAPD were extremely concerned. These guys were more than average bank robbers; they were psychopathic thrill-seekers. The authorities would have a hard time predicting when their next robbery would occur. Most bank robbers will rob when they run out of money. Drug addicts will go through pilfered money more quickly than other types of criminals. But the authorities had no clue when Phillips and Matasareanu might strike again.

Sometime after the aborted armored car attack, Phillips and Matasareanu saw the 1995 film *Heat,* staring Robert De Niro, Al Pacino, Tom Sizemore, and Val Kilmer. In the movie, De Niro, Sizemore, and Kilmer are bank robbers who botch the big heist. They end up taking on the entire Los Angeles Police Department in a running gun battle, using all the tools and skills of professional hit men. To the immature minds of Phillips and Matasarenu, this seemed like the next step to take.

On May 2, 1996, Phillips and Matasareanu burst into a Van Nuys Bank of America branch shortly after ten in the morning, with guns blazing. They both carried holstered sidearms, and they fired AK-47s, loaded with seventy-five-round drum magazines. They both wore black clothing and black ski masks, with sunglasses under the masks. They also wore black leather gloves and carried stopwatches. On top of that, both men were wearing body armor and combat vests, loaded with extra ammunition.

Matasareanu fired his armor-piercing bullets into the bandit-barrier door that led to a reinforced double-door room with bulletproof glass, smashing it to pieces. Once inside, he demanded that the bank manager open the vault. Matasareanu filled his duffel bag with money as Phillips terrified the customers, who were all lying face down on the floor. They walked slowly out of the bank, dragging the duffel bag to the same Chevrolet Celebrity they had used in the first Brinks robbery, which had been left in the parking lot with the engine running.

The bandits used their stopwatches, but only as decoration; they had taken six minutes to rob the bank, breaking Lamm's two-minute rule by four minutes. They had spent three times longer than was considered necessary to safely pull off a bank robbery.

Less than a month later, Phillips and Matasareanu pulled another bank robbery, exactly like the previous one, except this time it took place at the same bank where they gunned down Herman Cook. This time they took eight minutes to pull off the robbery, and they got away with $795,000.

Phillips and Matasareanu had over a million and a half dollars stashed in hiding places. They had rented a house for themselves so their wives would ask no questions about all the weapons and cash lying around. Being loners and losers, they had no mob connections through which to launder the money, and they had no idea how to use the large sum of money without arousing suspicion, although they bought some clothes and jewelry and rented better homes for their families.

Matasareanu, who was an epileptic, started having severe headaches, to the point that he suffered blackouts. He finally underwent an operation to relieve pressure on his brain, and it took months for him to recover. However, on February 28, 1997, Phillips and Matasareanu were ready to rob another Bank of America, this time on Laurel Canyon Drive in North Hollywood.

Shortly after nine in the morning, Phillips and Matasareanu burst into the bank, where they fired a couple of rounds into the ceiling and ordered everyone to the floor. After shattering the bandit-barrier door, they went about their business in their slow-motion style, much like during their previous two robberies. They even left the same white Chevy Celebrity in the parking lot, again with the engine running. But this time things were different. They had walked into the bank right in front of a passing LAPD patrol car.

The officers called in a report when they heard automatic weapon fire, and within a minute, the bank was surrounded by Los Angeles' "finest." Police procedure calls for officers to wait until the robbers are out of the bank before they challenge them, so they waited, incredibly for a full fifteen minutes.

Things weren't going well in the bank for Phillips and Matasareanu. Because of robbers' previous big hauls, Bank of America branches in the area had decided not to leave extremely large amounts of cash in their banks. Matasareanu screamed at the manager for more money. He even tried to loot the ATM machines, spraying them with automatic weapon fire. Phillips peeked out the door and spotted dozens of black and white LAPD cars surrounding the bank. He calmly walked back in to the bank. The misfits decided to make a stand.

As Phillips and Matasareanu walked through the

The bullet ridden body of bank robber Emil Dechebal Matasareanu awaits the coroner's wagon. *(Associated Press)*

bank's front door, dye packs inside the money-filled collapsible suitcase went off, making the $330,000 worthless. The robbers could have ended it right there and surrendered, but for reasons known only to Phillips and Matasareanu, perhaps inspired by the film *Heat* that they had watched so often, they decided to shoot it out with the entire LAPD.

Firing round after round of .223 tungsten-carbide bullets at every police officer and vehicle they saw, Phillips and Matasareanu had the police outgunned and pinned down. The police had 9-millimeter pistols and 12-gauge shotguns that were no match against fully automatic AK-47s. The police could see their bullets hitting the bandits, but they only knocked them back a bit and got their attention. Both cops and citizens hid behind anything that could conceal them, although many of them had been wounded and were bleeding.

Television station helicopters were on the scene, broadcasting the shootout live as it happened. At one point, Phillips aimed his rifle at a TV chopper and fired a burst at it.

Matasareanu got behind the wheel of the white Chevrolet, leaving the ruined money on the curb. Phillips didn't get into the car. Instead, he used the car as a shield, firing and reloading at will. After five minutes, Matasareanu put the car into drive and started moving, as Phillips walked beside it. Phillips then moved away from the safety of the vehicle, still firing his AK-47, and hid behind a parked semi-truck. His rifle jammed, so he dropped it and drew his 9-millimeter Beretta pistol and fired it at a group of officers. A well-aimed shot by an unknown police officer knocked the pistol out of Phillips' hand. Phillips picked up the gun, put it under his chin, and fired. At the exact same moment, a police bullet hit Phillips in the back of his neck. He died where he stood.

Meanwhile, Matasareanu drove slowly down residential streets. His car had four flat tires and the windows had been shattered by gunfire. The shot-up trunklid of the car bounced up and down. Matasareanu tried to block passing cars in hopes of hijacking one. He stopped a Jeep pickup, but the driver ran away, taking the keys with him.

Matasareanu didn't realize that there were no keys in the ignition until he had transferred his weapons into the Jeep. The fat man climbed out of the Jeep, just as a squad car full of cops came screaming up the street. Matasareanu took cover behind his beloved Chevy and started shooting at the squad car. The cops bailed out and fired on Matasareanu, shooting from numerous angles, including from under the vehicle.

Matasareanu was hit in the legs, and he threw his arms into the air to surrender. For reasons only Matasareanu knew, he then reached for his gun again and was slammed by dozens of bullets fired by the officers. The Romanian immigrant slowly fell to the pavement. The police took his weapons and handcuffed him. A detective asked the bleeding Matasareanu how he was doing. "Fuck you," he said. "Shoot me in the head." Matasareanu died shortly thereafter. Over 1,700 shots had been fired, with at least 1,100 fired by Phillips and Matasareanu. Nine LAPD officers, three civilians, and a dog were wounded by gunfire. Twelve LAPD patrol cars were destroyed, and eighty-five civilian cars were damaged.

The autopsy determined that Phillips had been hit nine times by bullets; two of these wounds would have been fatal. He was wearing forty-two pounds of body armor that covered his chest, back, arms, and legs. Matasareanu weighed in at 283 pounds, and he had suffered at least twenty-nine bullet wounds.

The results of the bankrobbers' blood tests came back positive for phenobarbital, a barbiturate used to treat epilepsy, hence the slow-motion fashion of the robbers.

Once the criminals were identified, the police raided their homes and found over $300,000 in stolen cash, a few weapons, and survivalist and bodybuilder magazines. They also found a well-worn videotape of *Heat*. The wives of the two criminals were completely clueless about their husbands' crimes and were not charged.

There are some people who believe that Matasareanu was purposely denied aid for his wounds and was allowed to bleed to death. With dozens of citizens and police officers wounded and in dire need of emergency attention, the health and safety of Matasareanu was probably the last thing on the minds of the officers who finally brought him down.

While on earth, Phillips and Matasareanu were social misfits and outcasts. Although these psychopaths each died under a hail of police bullets, surely God administered the final degree of justice.

Chapter 35

Eagle Scout Earns Merit Badge

Death Toll: 1

March 7, 2003, Ukiah—Mendocino County

Even today, both violence and justice can come swiftly on the streets of California cities.

On March 7, 2003, seventeen-year-old Julian Covella had no idea that his police ride-along would end up in one of the wildest shootouts in modern California history. The Eagle Scout and honor student was riding with Sergeant Marcus Young as part of the Explorer Scouts Police Cadet program when Young responded to a shoplifting complaint at the Ukiah Wal-Mart store about 9:00 P.M. The scout and the officer had never met before that night.

Sergeant Young had a female shoplifting suspect handcuffed and seated in the rear of his patrol car when the suspect's boyfriend, fugitive Neal Allan Beckman, approached the car and pulled a pistol out of his coat. Sergeant Young struggled to disarm Beckman, but the ex-con had the drop on him and shot him five times.

Young's bulletproof vest saved him from a fatal chest wound. Unfortunately, however, the fifteen-year veteran of the Ukiah Police Department was also hit in neck, cheek, shoulder, and left hand. Kneeling on the cold, dark parking lot and bleeding profusely, Young watch helplessly as Wal-Mart security guard Brett Schott jumped Beckman from behind, only to be stabbed in the ribs.

Julian Covella, who had taken cover behind a parked automobile, couldn't believe what was happening in front of him. Sergeant Young's right arm was paralyzed and his left hand had a bullet in it. Still kneeling, Young saw that Beckman was struggling to free the shotgun from its secured rack in the patrol car. Young shouted to Covella to help him pull out his sidearm. Covella ran to Young and, after a short effort that seemed like hours to the teenager, freed Young's pistol from the holster. After placing the gun in Young's bloody left hand, Covella helped steady Young's aim as he emptied his gun into Beckman, who was still trying to free the shotgun from its rack. Beckman lay bleeding in the front seat of the patrol car and died a short time later.

Beckman was thirty-five years old and had a criminal record in California and Idaho dating to the 1980s, when he was convicted of beating an elderly Willits man. He was wanted on a $100,000 Superior Court of California warrant after failing to make a midweek court appearance in connection with the beating and armed robbery of another elderly Ukiah man, who had later died of his injuries.

Sergeant Young, Schott, and Covella were hailed as heroes and one can only wonder what kind of merit badge Covella received from the Explorer Scouts. Their story made headlines across the country, leading to numerous appearances on talk shows.

Sometimes the good guys win through the assistance and brave actions of true citizen heroes.

Bibliography

Books

Atherton, Gertrude. *California: An Intimate History*. New York: Blue Ribbon Books, 1914.

Atkinson, Janet Irene. *Colorful Men and Women of the Mother Lode*. Sonora, CA: Jan Irene Publications, 2002.

Beers, Terry, ed. *Gunfight at Mussel Slough: Evolution of a Western Myth*. Berkeley, CA: Heyday Books, 2004.

Coblentz, Stanton A. *Villains and Vigilantes: The Story of James King of William and Power Justice in California*. New York: Thomas Yoseloff, Inc., 1936.

Convis, Charles L. *Frontier Vigilantes*. True Tales of the Old West series, vol. 17. Carson City, NV: Pioneer Press, 2001.

DeLeon, Richard Edward. *Left Coast City: Progressive Politics in San Francisco, 1975–1991*. Lawrence, KS: University of Kansas Press, 1992.

DeNevi, Don. *Western Train Robberies*. Millbrae, CA: Celestia Arts, 1976.

Dillinger, William C., ed. *A History of the Lower American River*, rev. ed. Carmichael, CA: American River Natural History Association, 1991.

Farrell, Harry. *Swift Justice*. New York: St. Martin's Press, 1992.

Fiorini-Jenner, Gail L., and Monica Jae Hall. *Western Siskiyou County*. The Making of America series. Charleston, SC: Arcadia Publishing, 2002.

Holden, William M. *Sacramento*. Fair Oaks, CA: Two Rivers Publishing, 1988.

Jackson, Joseph Henry. *Bad Company: The Story of California's Legendary and Actual Stage Robbers, Bandits, Highwaymen, and Outlaws from the Fifties to the Eighties*. N.p.: Bison Books, 1939.

Kyle, Douglas E., and Mildred Brooke Hoover, eds. *Historic Spots in California*. 5th ed. Stanford, CA: Stanford University Press, 2002.

LeBaron, Gaye. *Santa Rosa: A Nineteenth Century Town*. Santa Rosa, CA: Historia, Ltd., 1985.

Lyman, Palmer. *History of Mendocino County, California*. San Francisco: Alley, Bowen, and Co., 1880.

MacLean, Angus. *Legends of the California Bandidos*. Sanger, CA: Word Dancer Press, 2004.

Mather, R. E., and F. E. Boswell. *Gold Camp Desperadoes: A Study of Violence, Crime, and Punishment on the Mining Frontier*. Norman and London: University of Oklahoma Press, 1993.

McMurry, Alan. *Just a Little Lynching Now and Then*. Yreka, CA: Alan J. McMurry, 1988.

Metz, Leon Claire. *The Encyclopedia of Lawmen, Outlaws, and Gunfighters*. New York: Checkmark Books, 2003.

Monahan, Sherry. *The Wicked West: Boozers, Cruisers, Gamblers, and More*. Tucson: Rio Nuevo Publishers, 2005.

Mungo, Ray. *San Francisco Confidential: Tales of Scandal and Excess from the Town That's Seen Everything*. New York: Birch Lane Press, 1995.

Nash, Jay Robert. *Bloodletters and Badmen*. New York: M. Evans and Company, 1973.

——. *The Encyclopedia of Western Lawmen and Outlaws*. n.p.: Da Capo Press, 1994.

Newton, Michael. *The Encyclopedia of Conspiracies and Conspiracy Theories*. New York: Checkmark Books, 2006.

———. *The Encyclopedia of Kidnappings*. New York: Checkmark Books, 2002.

———. *The Encyclopedia of Robberies, Heists, and Capers*. New York: Checkmark Books, 2002.

Pfeifer, Michael J. *Rough Justice: Lynching and American Society, 1874–1947*. Champaign, IL: University of Illinois Press, 2004.

Pryor, Alton. *Little Known Tales in California History*. Roseville, CA: Stagecoach Publishing, 1997.

Reasoner, James. *Draw: The Greatest Gunfights of the American West*. New York: Berkley Books, 2003.

Rehder, William J., and Gordon Dillow. *Where the Money Is: True Tales from the Bank Robbery Capital of the World*. New York: W. W. Norton & Company, 2003.

Richards, Rand. *Historic San Francisco: A Concise History and Guide*. San Francisco: Heritage House Press, 2003.

Rogers, Justus H. *Colusa County*. Orland, CA: n.p., 1891.

Secrest, William B. *California Desperadoes: Stories of Early California Outlaws in Their Own Words*. Sanger, CA: Word Dancer Press, 2000.

———. *California Feuds: Vengeance, Vendettas, and Violence on the Old West Coast*. Sanger, CA: Word Dancer Press, 2005.

———. *Dark and Tangled Threads of Crime: San Francisco's Famous Police Detective, Isaiah W. Lees*. Sanger, CA: Word Dancer Press, 2004.

Shilts, Randy. *The Mayor of Castro Street: The Life and Times of Harvey Milk*. Cartersville, CA: Addison-Wesley, 1984.

Sifakis, Carl. *The Encyclopedia of American Crime*. New York: Smithmark, 1992.

Smith, Jesse M. *Sketches of Old Sacramento: A Tribute to Joseph A. McGowan*. Sacramento: Sacramento County Historical Society, 1976.

Stewart, George R. *Committee of Vigilance: Revolution in San Francisco, 1851*. Boston: Houghton Mifflin Company, 1964.

Swierczynsky, Duane. *This Here's a Stick Up: The Big, Bad Book of American Bank Robbery*. Indianapolis: Alpha, 2002.

Periodicals & Journals

Bedau, Hugo Adam, and Michael L. Radelet. "Miscarriages of Justice in Potentially Capital Cases," *Stanford Law Review* 40 (November 1987): 100.

Edwards, Harold L. "Ambush at Long Tom," *True West* (November 1992).

Journal of the Sonoma County Historical Society.

Wagon Wheels—Journal of the Colusa County Historical Society.

Newspapers

Bakersfield *Californian*

Colusa Sun (Colusa, CA)

Humboldt Daily Times (Eureka, CA)

Kern County Weekly Courier (Bakersfield, CA)

Mendocino Dispatch Democrat (Ukiah, CA)

Press Democrat (Ukiah, CA)

New York Times

Sacramento Daily Bee

Sacramento Daily Record-Union

Sacramento Daily Union

San Francisco Chronicle

San Francisco Examiner

San Jose Mercury News

Scotts Valley News (Scotts Valley, CA)

Siskiyou Daily News (Yreka, CA)

Siskiyou Pioneer (Yreka, CA)

Yreka Journal Extra

Website

crimelibrary.com/terrorists_spies/assassins/kennedy/1.html. Joseph Geringer, Courtoom Television Network LLC.

Index

About the Author

Jennifer King

David A. Kulczyk is a Sacramento based freelance writer and award-winning author of short fiction. His work has appeared in the *Sacramento News and Review, Chico News and Review, East Bay Express*, and *SF Guardian*. He is also an associate editor for *Maximum Ink Music* magazine.

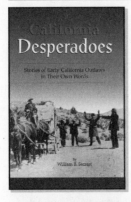

CALIFORNIA DESPERADOES

Stories of Early California Outlaws in Their Own Words
by William B. Secrest

> "Fascinating..."
> — John Boessenecker,
> author of *Gold Dust and Gunsmoke*

$15.95
Printed two-color throughout
Many rare photographs & illustrations
Bibliography • Index
272 pages • 6" x 9" • ISBN 1-884995-19-5

FROM MUD-FLAT COVE TO GOLD TO STATEHOOD

California 1840-1850
by Irving Stone
With a foreword by Jean Stone

> Irving Stone *"...one of America's foremost
> literary figures and its greatest story teller."*

> *"...a fascinating book for high school students and adults."*
> —*The Bookhandler*

$12.95
176 pages • 6" x 9" • ISBN 1-884995-17-9

THE NEWHALL INCIDENT

America's Worst Uniformed Cop Massacre
by Chief John Anderson with Marsh Cassady

> *"Not since Truman Capote's* In Cold Blood *has there been a
> true crime story that so intimately captures the lives of
> killers, victims and police."*
> — Ted Schwarz, author of *The Hillside Strangler*

$14.95
With never-before published CHP photographs
192 pages • 6" x 9" • ISBN 1-884956-01-7

SAN JUAN BAUTISTA

The Town, The Mission & The Park
by Charles W. Clough

> "Highly recommended."
> —*The Bookwatch*

$18.95
175 historic photos, maps and other illustrations
Bibliography • Index
144 pages • 8½" x 11" • ISBN 1-884995-07-1

Available from bookstores, on-line bookstores or by calling 1-800-497-4909